WAKING UP

It takes but one moment in your life that you find yourself

WAKING UP

*Lessons Learned Through My Adventures
with Life and Breast Cancer*

Thanks for an awesome tour!

Safe travels –

Anne Dennish

ANNE DENNISH

Copyright © 2016 by Anne Dennish.

Library of Congress Control Number:		2016903204
ISBN:	Hardcover	978-1-5144-6723-7
	Softcover	978-1-5144-6724-4
	eBook	978-1-5144-6725-1

All rights reserved. No part of this book may be reproduced or transmitted in any form or by any means, electronic or mechanical, including photocopying, recording, or by any information storage and retrieval system, without permission in writing from the copyright owner.

Any people depicted in stock imagery provided by Thinkstock are models, and such images are being used for illustrative purposes only.
Certain stock imagery © Thinkstock.

Print information available on the last page.

Rev. date: 02/23/2016

To order additional copies of this book, contact:
Xlibris
1-888-795-4274
www.Xlibris.com
Orders@Xlibris.com
636853

CONTENTS

Introduction xiii

LESSONS LEARNED THROUGH MY ADVENTURES WITH LIFE

"First and Foremost: Find Your Funny" 1
"When Social Networking Becomes Social Not Working" 3
"Giving Your Day Away" 6
"I'm Having a Girl Moment" 8
"What Makes a Man a Man" 10
"A Little Crazy Goes A Long Way in a Day!" 13
"The Naked Truth About Being Naked!" 15
"Dreaming" 17
"Those That Dare" 19
"The Waiting Game" 21
"The Differences: Embrace Them or Replace Them" 23
"Be the Doorbell, Not the Doormat" 26
"Down the Explain Drain" 28
"Caution: Don't Feed The Ego!" 31
"I'm Sorry, But I'm Not" 34
"Free Will" 36
"The Discomfort Zone" 38
"Don't Shoot Your I Out" 40
"The True Colors of Relationships" 43
"Life After Life After Life" 47
"The Mind of a Heart" 49
"What is Love?" 51
"The Ghosts of Relationships Past" 53
"A State of Affairs" 55
"Sometimes We Go Back" 59
"Why Wasn't I Good Enough" 61
"Ignorance and Bliss" 64
"Pulling the Trigger" 67

"It's Time to Say Good-Bye" 69
"Letting Go" 71
"Moving Forward" 75
"The Truth Seeker" 77
"Thinking" 79
"The Ultimate Test of Trust" 81
"Time Frame" 84
"Beautiful Boy" 88
"Fallen Angel" 91
"Grief Stricken" 93
"Under the Tree" 95
"A Letter to My Children" 96
"Ruthless People" 98
"Preach It, Teach It…Then Reach for It" 100
"Caution: You're About to Make a Memory" 102
"I Wish I Had Never…" 105
"The Voice of the Ocean" 108
"Beliefs" 111

LESSONS LEARNED THROUGH MY ADVENTURES WITH BREAST CANCER

"A Note from the Author" 117
"A Bump in the Road to My Happiness…Day One" 119
"A Bump on the Road to My Happiness… Day Two" 121
"A Bump on the Road to My Happiness… Day Three" 122
"Biopsy Day for the Bump in My Road to Happiness" 123
"Biopsy… Done!" 124
"It's More Than A Bump in the Road to My Happiness" 126
"The Unveiling" 128
"For Today, There's Peace" 130
"Anxiously Awaiting" 131
"The Waiting is Over; The Results Are In" 132
"A Glimmer of Hope" 134
"Taking the Day Off" 136
"Just When You Thought It Was Safe… WTF!" 137
"Those Who Matter Don't Mind" 138
"This Is The Time of My Life" 139
"It's All In Your Perspective" 140
"Save The Date" 142

"When Your Breasts' Do The Talking!" 144
"Second Opinions Lead to Different Decisions" 146
"Oh, The Things You Will Think When You Have Cancer!" 149
"My Point of Impact" 151
"The Pro's and Con's of Cancer!" 153
"My Mountain is Waiting…Tomorrow's the Day" 155
"And The Climb Has Begun…" 157
"Life Still Goes On" 159
"You Can Always Change, No Matter Your Age" 160
"It's Like An Arranged Marriage" 163
"Behind the Wheel at Wall Stadium!" 164
"Charlotte's Web…Make that Anne's Web!" 167
"The Breast Cancer Club" 169
"Breast Cancer… The Time Warp" 171
"Home is Where…" 173
"If These Wigs Could Talk" 174
"The Surgery" 176
"53 and Cancer-Free!" 178
"Last Day of Radiation" 179
"Last Treatment" 181
"My Port-O-Call Girl" 182
"Now What?" 183
"Fits Like a Glove" 185
"The Lessons of the Adventures" 188
"Before I say good-bye…" 192

With love and gratitude to:

My children: Eric, Emma, Dan, Noah and Sam

My love, Rob Contreras

My closest tribe of friends: Lesley, Liz, Terilyn and Colleen

My Angel girls:

Bobbi, Maura, Ann, Robin, Livie, Diane, Sysco, Linda, Doreen & Delaney

You've been an inspiration to me and this book was possible

because of each and every one of you.

~Anne Dennish~

~This book is dedicated to the people who put me through hell, only to make me realize who the people are that make me feel like I'm in heaven.~

Introduction

This book was born out of heartache, heartbreak, lies, truth, friends showing their true colors, and from my journey with breast cancer.

It's not a book of pity or one that requires sympathy; while it may have been born out of "not so good experiences," it taught me a lot about who I am, how strong I am, and most importantly, it taught me how to love myself.

It doesn't really matter what it was born out of; what matters is that it's alive and kicking! This book is here to make a difference to someone who has been through what I have or has found themselves in situations similar to my own.

I don't mind having gone through rough times or cancer; I simply don't want it to have been in vain. I believe all things, good and bad, happen for a reason, and if this book was one of them, then all I have gone through had a purpose: to inspire, heal, or give a new perspective to someone who may need one.

My hope is that this book will touch at least one person and change their life for the better, because if I can do that, I'll know the reason that this book was "born;" and I'll know the reason that I was "born" too!

With love,

~Anne Dennish~

"A dreamer is a realist with faith."

Anne Dennish

"One day I woke up, changed my direction, and wrote this book about the journey."

Lessons Learned Through My Adventures With Life

"First and Foremost: Find Your Funny"

As I was putting this book together, I was wondering which story to begin it with. Many thoughts crossed my mind as to "the right" story, and through all that thinking and wondering I remembered the one thing I always tell people who are going through a difficult time: "find your funny."

So, as I begin this very first chapter of "Waking Up," I say to you, no matter what difficult situation you are in, around, or working through, it's so important to "find your funny" in it, and that's what you will find as you read this book, that no matter what situation I'm writing about, the best way to deal with it is to find something funny in it. If you can learn to do this, you will attack and handle every situation that comes your way with grace, dignity, and a good laugh or two! It's in the darkest times that we need to remember the power of laughter, the intent of a smile, the sweetness of accepting what is, and what we can do about it. Laughing through something doesn't make it less important in your life; laughing makes it easier to handle.

I'm not saying that it's always easy to do, and sometimes it takes some time before you're able to look back on something and find its' funny, yet what I'm saying is that it can be done, even for some of the worst situations.

I had to find my funny when I lost my hair from chemo. I knew that morning that it was beginning to fall out in strands, so I cried a little bit and slept throughout most of the day. I kept reminding myself that I had to find my funny, even though at the time this wasn't funny to me at all. So, as you'll read in "Forget Charlottes' Web" near the end of this book, I found my funny in the car with my son, as strand upon strand was blowing throughout the car. The funny came about when he thought it was a spider web, only to realize it was my hair! There was my funny!

There's times when you have a day that everything and anything can go wrong! It's difficult when one thing after another happens all at once, yet you can find your funny. When people say to me "what are the odds" I always answer: "in my life, very good!" We both get a chuckle from that.

Divorce? Well, I'm divorced twice, and my funny there is that I will tell people that breast cancer was easier than two divorces; at least with the cancer, you know going in what you're up against and what had to be done. Divorce? Not so much! See, there's a little funny in a not so funny situation.

I know that there are times that tears need to be shed, hearts will be broken, and we will feel hurt or sadness through difficult times. That's normal and healthy, yet my whole theory behind "finding your funny" is that it's alright to laugh, to smile, to even joke about all those situations and feelings you're going through. To me, once you've gone through it, or while still in it, if you can find your funny then you have found your strength, and you will have known you've gotten through it.

Laughter is truly the best medicine, and life is all about our perspective. Change what you can and make peace with what you can't. Life happens to us all, and we're all in this together, learning and growing throughout this journey we call "life." And above all else, remember this:

"First and foremost, find your funny!"

"When Social Networking Becomes Social Not Working"

I would bet that most of you reading this book are, or have been, part of a social networking site. It's a rare occasion that I meet someone who isn't. There seems to be so many avenues of social networking all over the internet lately; depending on your age usually determines which site you're a player on.

Yet first, let me be perfectly clear about something: I am not bashing these sites whatsoever; I am part of a few myself. What I will say is that, as a writer and avid people watcher, I have paid close attention to these sites and the actions of the people on them. It's actually intriguing when you begin to analyze and watch with a different perspective; "objectively" watching, that is.

There's good and bad with social networking, and I've been on both sides of the coin. I think that they can be a wonderful tool at keeping friends and family closely connected, especially when the distance between them requires a plane ticket or mass transit. It's wonderful for business and causes; it's great for invitations to social events that you're a part of; it's even important when those in need require help from others. That's the best part of it all; it keeps us all connected and up to date on what our friends and family are doing.

Now for the "not so good" side of it, and this is one I apprehensively write about, as I don't want to offend my friends or family by expressing my observations. However, with that being said, I've seen or heard of sites being the catalyst that can ruin friendships, relationships, and even marriages. I've seen and heard about it happening. The sad part is that the site itself is not the cause, it's the person who uses it for all the wrong reasons. We've heard of the "stalkers" on it, and just when you think you know all the people on your site, you find out that some use fake names to watch what you're doing; some hack your account. This is the downside of the internet: we expose ourselves to everyone on the internet, no matter how cautious you are or how locked in you believe your personal site to be. When used for the wrong reasons, it can cause some major problems within your life, and isn't that ironic that this "on line life" we have can cross right into your "real life."

For example, if you wouldn't cheat on someone in real life, why would you do it on the internet? If you wouldn't tell someone off in real life, why would you do it on your site? I believe the problem is that we tend to think that the rules in life are different than the rules of the internet, and this is so not true! The boundaries you have in your life should be the same, yet I watch all these people making comments, or constantly "liking" something that they have no business doing. "Trust" in a healthy relationship can become an issue through the internet. Most people don't share passwords, so this is one big leap of faith and trust!

One of the biggest things I've been watching lately is what and who certain people like and what they don't. I've noticed that someone will always like a member of the opposite sexes post, yet won't like a post if their spouse or significant other is in it. It's almost as if they're defying the other party in this couple by making a statement, which is: "I had him/her first, and I'm not going to like anything with you in it, just him/her." Most people like that wouldn't take the time or have the nerve in the real world to make that statement, yet hand them a computer and let "their" games begin. It may not seem like much to some, yet to others and myself, it's annoying, can be hurtful, and just plain pisses you off!

You can "look," but don't' "like."

If you feel the need to stalk or look at all of someone's personal business on their site, remember that once you "like" it, everyone, not just that person, will know that you did. This can inevitably become a problem in a relationship. It's not much different that being out with someone (in person, that is) and noticing them ignoring you, or flirting with someone else; you don't like it if someone is hitting on your spouse or significant other while you're standing there, yet that's my point: what you see in person can actually be seen on-line as well, all by the constant "liking/commenting" on someone...especially if you're always doing it to one particular someone. That's the problem; what's hurtful or bothersome in the "real" world is considered to be "no big deal" on the internet. If you believe that, you're kidding yourself. You're giving yourself permission to be ignorant. Just as "real" life affairs begin by a few phone calls or harmless visits, an "internet" one begins with "liking and/or commenting" to one person far too much, and then it crosses the line to private messages. Lines of intimacy on-line can be crossed this very way, and if you're in a relationship that means something to you, remember that the internet is the internet; it's not that person who holds your hand, snuggles with you at night, or tells you they love you.

"To inter-net or inter-not; that is the question!"

The other problem with the "liking" key is that if you don't like someone's post which may have someone in it you don't like, trust me, they'll notice.

WAKING UP

I have watched so many people live almost their entire existence on these sites; that's how they measure their self-esteem, by the number of "likes and/or comments!" It's become sad that the real world is becoming a thing of the past, and that "living in the moment" is becoming "living on line!" I've seen affairs happening from them, as well as a break-down of friendships. I lost two close friends through social media, yet it was two people who forgot what interaction with an actual human was like, whether it was in person or by phone. These two people counted their "likes and comments" daily, and felt that they were in intimate friendships with everyone they connected with. That's not true, yet that's what happened to me.

There's no real intimacy on line, just typing, sending, and liking. Personally, I like a voice on the phone and a body next to me; that's the real world. The internet world should simply be the perk to it; that extra tool we have to keep in touch, send a quick message or inspirational thought to someone.

It's all really about the intimacy of relationships, and while we wouldn't cross a line or jeopardize them in the real world, many find the courage to do so on-line. It's not healthy or more importantly, not "truth" to be someone you're not on-line. It's not right to step over boundaries that are set in the real world, to be selfish enough to jeopardize someone else's relationships with family, friends or a significant other simply because you have yourself fooled into believing that it's okay to do it on-line, even though you wouldn't think of doing it in the "real" world.

Think before you "like" and when all else fails, if you feel the need to stalk or constantly look someone up to see what they're doing, remember: "look but don't like."

Just that one click of a key can ruin something that means the world to someone else, so be careful to "think before you click!"

One last piece of advice: what goes around comes around, and the truth is that karma is a bitch, and she most definitely exists on-line and in the real world.

"Giving Your Day Away"

"Stop and smell the roses" is a familiar term to most, yet one so often forgotten. Life can get busy, and we forget to take some time in each day to stop and appreciate all that our life has to offer. Yet sometimes a day flies by, and before long we realize it's ended before we ever started it. You wonder where your day went, and you have to ask yourself this: "why did I just give my day away?"

The answer isn't always simple, yet it's usually the same: you let it slip away to other people, places and things. You forgot to keep some of the day for yourself.

Life can be busy, and new adventures are to be found at some of the most unexpected times, yet we still have to remember to keep some of the day for ourselves. Yes, life throws a curve ball now and again, and the most carefully planned day spirals into the opposite direction. It's easier to follow the curveballs spinning into thin air than to catch them, handle them, and keep going.

Fatigue plays a big part in losing your day; physical fatigue, and the worst of all, mental fatigue, are the biggest thieves in taking your day away. All valid reasons, yet the point in keeping a healthy life is to not allow that to happen… at least not too often.

Life is about balance, and there are days that the balance seems too far out of reach. Yet it's important to find it, and more importantly, to recognize when you're losing it, as that helps with all the fatigue thieves that step in and grab the day from you.

So how do you keep that balance? There are many ways. The most important step is finding a few moments each day, preferably in the morning, to get yourself grounded. Stand outside on the sand or grass, close your eyes, take a deep breath, and envision a white light of energy coming up from the ground, through your toes, up to the top of your head. It's like a natural boost of energy which requires as little as five or ten minutes of your time. It's well worth the effort and as stimulating as that first rush you get from your morning coffee.

Another practice is to meditate in a sacred space, your "quiet" space, or your most "happy" place. For some it's a room in your home, for others it's outside under the sun or moon. For those lucky enough to live near the water, there's nothing better than grounding yourself with your toes in the sand. Whether you choose to call it meditation or prayer, the point is to find a few minutes of quiet to gather your thoughts, remove all negative thoughts from your thinking, and

WAKING UP

replace them with the energy of positive thoughts and intentions. Breathe, close your eyes, and envision yourself well rested, healthy and in balance.

You'll find that it's very simple to gather your thoughts once you find the ritual that works for you. In time, you'll rely on this ritual to ground yourself everyday and find the balance you so deserve.

Once you are able to do this, you will find much more of the day within your hands and not the hands of someone else. You'll find you need less coffee and enjoy drinking more water. You're body will find a deeper sleep at night, and an easier awakening in the morning. Before long, balance is no longer something you have to find, but a way that you live.

All things we do in life should be for our highest good, and those around you will enjoy the benefits of the balanced you just as much as you do.

Take time to keep the day "yours," one that you willingly share with others, not something that was stolen away.

Stop and feel the sun on your face…

Breathe in the ocean air…

Marvel at the clear night sky filled with stars…

Sit in wonder at the sight of the mountains…

Embrace the warmth, snuggle into the cold…

Listen to the laughter of others…

See the smiles of happiness on those you love…

Enjoy foods that make your body feel good…

Appreciate the friendships of those within your circle…

And most importantly, stop and smell the roses.

If you can find your balance you will have found your day, and no one will ever take it from you again.

"I'm Having a Girl Moment"

I'd like to consider myself a strong woman. I've weathered many storms, right along with breast cancer, so I'd say I'm pretty tough. Yet there are those moments I stop myself and have to admit that I'm having a "girl" moment.

Ugh…now everyone will see I'm human, and worse yet, that I'm a "girl!" Just great! Then again, maybe it is great.

Why do we feel, as women, that we have to be strong all the time? Why can't we have those moments of being a "girl?" Better yet, why aren't we allowed to?

It's because that's what society and the world has taught us; only the strong survive. Yet even the weakest of a soul will survive when they find they're strength.

Society has looked at women as the sex that will cry, get jealous, have fits of PMS, and the list goes on. And that list is okay. It really is. We just forget that when feelings that we view as weak, compared to our feelings of strength surface, we feel as though we've lost it…our minds, that is. We sit there with this foreign feeling of tears and jealousy (because when you're strong you never feel any less!) We feel insecure, we feel scared, and those are the feelings of a "girl" because that's what most of society thinks of women.

We're only now, in the last several decades, making strides to be accepted as strong women. Yet I have to be honest, I feel at times we've surpassed being strong and taken it to another level. That's why when those "girl" feelings surface, people look at us like we have two heads. They give us that look of "Who ARE you?" They know us as strong, WE know us as strong, and truth is, I believe we are more surprised at our "girl moments" than the person on the other end of it.

So how do you handle those sporadic "girl moments?" You do it with grace and dignity, much deep breathing, and accept that this too shall pass, because after all, you are a "girl." And there's no shame in that. You just need to balance the strong woman with the girl tucked deep inside from another time in your life. Accept her, embrace her, and love her, because it was that "girl" that was instrumental in making you the strong woman you are today.

Love her insecurities, her tears, her fears, and be grateful for the lessons that all of that taught you. She taught you how to be a lady, and was there for you

WAKING UP

when you needed to find the strength in your time of weakness. She let you cry silently to yourself when you were hurt, and let you feel afraid when the darkness overshadowed the light. She grew up and along side of you, and the woman you are now, is the woman that is ever changing to become the woman you longed to be.

Society may not always understand the "girl" moments that creep into our present self, yet you understand. Smile silently at those jealous pangs over a new beau, cleanse your soul in the tears of heartbreak, and hold tight to the fears that may pop into your life, because those fears have a lesson to teach you as well, and with each fear we find ourselves staring face to face with, a new strength will be found.

Strong women are created from the "girl" moments of our life, and the balance of the two is an amazing combination. There's no win or lose in that, only a greater story on the journey of our life.

Enjoy the occasional "girl" moment and be brave enough to let the rest of the world enjoy that "girl" as well!

"What Makes a Man a Man"

The world today places a description on everything and everyone. We tend to lose sight of who we truly are and instead we morph into who we believe we're supposed to be. We fall into the "role" of mommy, lover, father, and friend…the list goes on. Yet those of us who strive to be independent have to take that leap of faith that is called strength: the strength to be who we are.

As young women, our idea of what a "man" is supposed to be was based on the men we grew up with: our fathers, brothers, or perhaps an uncle or grandfather. Yet as we've matured and grown up, the question of "what is a man" comes up more and more frequently amongst girlfriends. It can make for quite an interesting conversations, although maybe the question should be: "what makes a man a man?"

I can only speak from personal experience and my own thoughts on this, having been raised by a dad, had three brothers and four sons, and survived two divorces and a not so good 2 year relationship. I'd say those experiences should count for something! I consider myself a strong woman and credit that to having had to be strong based on my relationships with all these "men." I've learned to joke about it, although it is more a sarcastic statement of truth when I say: I'd like to meet a man who's more man than me. And let me say this: he's hard to find.

I believe that as women we all have our own perspective on what a "man" truly is. There are some that may believe that the qualities that make a "man a man" is his physical strength and the ability to protect us under any circumstance. He's the one who shields us from the bad, and wants us to see only the good.

That's not my belief, and truth be told, it's not the belief of other women I've spoken to. It seems that the older we get the idea of what makes a "man a man" matures. Suddenly, that old high school way of thinking that "my boyfriend beat someone up that was messing with me" is no longer our thinking. In fact, as we mature, that perception we once had in high school looks immature and silly.

I've come to see that as I've watched and known many different men over the years, that the men who still have that mentality are the ones that lack self-esteem, direction, and have a few truths about themselves that they're unwilling to face. This is what makes them still look like high school boys. They're not bad guys, or the guy we wouldn't give a second look at, yet they become the guy we find ourselves helping to get them to see their truths, and what we become to them is somewhat of a "mother." Once that happens, I will tell you, there's not much hope for a relationship. The moment we feel and act as if we're mothering them, it's nearly impossible to find that relationship as wife or girlfriend.

There are many qualities that make them a "man," and while not all are the same, this is the similar qualities we all feel makes a "man" a real "man:"

- **He's willing to protect a woman under an abusive situation, using physical force ONLY if necessary, yet always choosing to solve a problem with his intelligence and voice.**

- **He's not afraid to show his softer, emotional side. When he's hurt, he has no problem expressing this through words and tears, if need be. He's willing to show a woman that he can be as vulnerable as she is.**

- **A woman's tears' make him stop in his tracks, whether she is wrong or not. He's willing to put aside his own feelings to comfort her, hold her, and tell her that everything will be okay.**

- **He may not always understand what a woman is saying or trying to express, yet he will make every attempt to try. He's won't be so stubborn as to not listen, but a "man" will try his best to hear what a woman has to say, and if he doesn't understand, he'll admit that honestly and not judge her**

- **A real man knows instinctively how to love his woman, through the ups and downs, the good times and bad.**

- **A real man is strong when his woman can't be, and he allows her to be strong when he can't, and that is the most "man" he can be; when he admits his weaknesses, and doesn't constantly force his "strengths" down your throat.**

- **A real man knows he loves his woman, yet if she doesn't feel it and expresses that to him, he will do whatever it takes to make her feel loved.**

- **And most importantly: A REAL MAN PUTS DOWN HIS PHONE WHEN HE'S WITH HER.**

ANNE DENNISH

You may or may not agree with all of the above, yet you'll probably agree with a handful of them. The bottom line is a real man isn't afraid to feel; to feel sad, weak, or afraid. A real man trusts the woman he loves to see all of him, and a real woman lets him.

"A Little Crazy Goes A Long Way in a Day!"

Some days we get in our own way. It's those days we wake up and feel tired, with no energy to do much of anything. We might be feeling sad and not know why, or genuinely not feel like our usual self. We all have 'em, myself included, yet I won't allow myself to have them often. It could be that I woke up after having a restless sleep the night before, or it's a gray day without sun, or it could be that I didn't like how my first cup of coffee tasted. The reason doesn't matter; what matters is that you're feeling it. So what do you do with a day like this? I've got an idea…

You sway, your twirl, you dance, you slide down the halls in your socks; in other words, you step out of your own way, get a bit selfish and silly, and do something FUN!

I used to hate these "pity party" kind of days, until I realized and accepted that they are a necessary part of our journey of learning more about ourselves. Imagine if your life was perfect and you never felt anything less than happy; how in the world would you recognize something you already feel, if you didn't have a day of feeling less than that?

"Trials, tribulations and blessings are one in the same, because you can't have one without the other."

I believe there's a reason for every down day you encounter. It's our body and souls' way of letting us know we're not taking care of ourselves, or paying attention to our intuition. The Universe kicks our ass every so often when we're "not paying attention." Don't think it's a bad day because you did something wrong; look at it as a day you needed to stop and breathe, pay more attention to your health, listen to your intuition, or simply "be." It's a day the Universe is telling you that you need to "learn something."

We tell our children that "learning can be fun," don't we? We hear their grumbles and complaints about school and homework, yet we tell them to make the best of it, make it fun, and that tomorrow is another day. So, why don't we tell ourselves to make the best of it? Why don't we remind ourselves that tomorrow is another day? It's because we think we're too old for that kind thinking, yet that's not true at all. In fact, that's the exact kind of thinking we should be having on a down day! There's no age limit on fun… at least I don't think there is! I know it's certainly not written in my book or entertained in my own way of thinking!

What do you do for your kids or a friend when they're down? Let me guess: you try and cheer them up or make them laugh, right? Alright, then here's a new concept to think about: do it for yourself! You won't always have someone around to cheer you up, so pick something you like do, and be silly! Turn up your favorite, upbeat music, and let loose! Twirl, dance, sway, even slide across the floor in your socks! I can tell you from personal experience that it works every time, especially the "sock sliding!"

"Silly soothes the soul!"

Adults spend so much time trying to figure it all out and keep it all together, that every once in awhile we just have to step out of that role of "adult" and simply be "you!" It's okay to be silly, because silly is what let's your heart be happy, no matter what is going on around you.

Trust me, no one's life is perfect. We're all on a different journey, but no ones' experiences are any less than our own, or any more for that fact. Embrace the challenges, accept the down days, and celebrate the life you have, because as we all know, life can change in an instant.

People often ask me "how are you still standing after all the crazy things that have happened to you in your life?" My answer: "I've always been standing; all those experiences just made me stand stronger… and dance a lot more!"

"The Naked Truth About Being Naked!"

Most people I know have a Bucket List. It's that little list we carry in our mind of all the things we want to do before we die. It's also that list of things that we want to do, but all too often, we're afraid to do. We make excuses of not having the time to do it, or we simply don't think it's important enough to do. At this stage of my life it's my list of "do it and get it done!" So now I'm doing as much as I can and regretting nothing!

Life is short enough, isn't it? Why fantasize about what we want to do? Why just carry a list in our mind? Shouldn't we all have the freedom to be who we are? There's no such thing as an "alter ego" in us. It's just our "true-self" coming out!

So, I went on a vacation. Some called it spontaneous, reckless, and even selfish. I called it much-needed fun and a matter of survival! Truth be told, it was more fun than I had imagined, and I did manage to knock quite a few things off my Bucket List! It was my alter ego in full swing…literally. It was and still is, the "real" me, and I couldn't be happier with the person I found and allowed myself to become!

When finding the true you inside, there are times we must find the true you on the outside. In my case, I bared it all: body and soul. It was quite an experience and the most comfortable, content feeling I have felt in years with my own body, and of course, my own soul. No more speaking in code to those of you who haven't figured it out yet: I went to a nude beach. Not just once, or even twice, but every single day of my vacation. The truth is, I loved it! It was freedom at its best: no hiding, shame or embarrassment involved. It was, simply put: wonderful!

There were many people on that beach, all sizes and shapes, all comfortable in their own skin, which helped to make me more comfortable in mine! The first day on the beach I stuck to my chair, allowing myself to get to know the lay of the land. I sat people watching, and getting used to this new-found freedom. By the second day, and every day thereafter, I was up and about walking around, talking to everyone else there! Strangely enough, new friends were made, and there was quite the camaraderie among us all. I stepped into the world of nakedness, holding the most fun, intriguing conversations with other naked people. I wondered how I'd feel when I was home and had to step out of nakedness. The greatest part of it all is that no one seems to notice that anyone IS naked. The funniest part was seeing them out at night and noticing that they weren't naked!

ANNE DENNISH

In the world of "clothed" people, you can tell a lot about them by what they're wearing, how their hair looks, even by the jewelry they have on. The status of their life is blatantly worn on them. On a nude beach, however, there is no status to be seen. There's no way to look at someone and know much about them at all, except that they're as free-spirited as you. That's the beauty of it, you simply get to know them by talking to them, not by looking at them.

I wore my new bathing suit the day before I came home for less than an hour. It felt invasive to be so "covered" up after having been so "exposed," yet, there are times when we have to conform and accept the ways of the "real" world. We have to wear clothes!

Vacation is over, the beach I fell in love with is now a million miles away, but the experience will live with me for a lifetime! When the weather is dreary, or the day getting rough, I just close my eyes and let my thoughts wander back to that wonderful trip, and that time on the beach where I truly could be myself. I loved the "naked truth" of that beach because it brought out more of the "naked truth" about me.

"Dreaming"

Since the day they could understand the English language, I've taught my children that it's alright to dream; to want something you may think you can't have. I've taught them that it's okay to dream for those things, because in the end, whether you've caught a dream or not, at the very least you had one! You took a chance, jumped into faith, and gave it all you've got to see if you could get there. At the very most, you caught your dream and at the very least, you learned something about yourself. The point is this: you'll never know until you've tried. I've taught them never to regret anything in their life that happens, because ultimately all things happen to teach us more about ourselves. I've also taught them that the only regret they will ever have is not reaching for their dream.

"Dreaming is the ability to see in ourselves that which no one else can."

That regret will teach them one thing: that they didn't have enough faith in themselves to take a chance.

Life is about taking chances, taking a risk every once in awhile and dreaming as big as you can. I've had moments of wondering if my dreams were too big, if I'm going for something that couldn't possibly happen; then I think about all the stories of those people who dreamed just as big as I have. Some of their dreams came true; sometimes even larger than they had imagined.

The dreamers are our inspiration; they show us that they were once ordinary people who became extraordinary by taking a chance in a leap of faith towards their dream. They are the "doers" and "the dreamers."

"Failure is staying within your comfort zone;

Success is stepping out of it."

Not every dream we have will come true, yet we become better people when we pursue them. We learn more about ourselves; we become less fearful to take a chance; we become stronger. So why not become a dreamer? It's quite a powerful place to be. It's all about "us" not "them." It's about our wants and needs, and not those of someone else. It doesn't limit us, it enlarges us. It doesn't keep us wrapped tightly in a box, but allows us to push ourselves out of it. Dreaming is the ability to see in ourselves what no one else can; it is our highest form of our "true self."

"A dreamer is a realist with faith."

"Dreamers" aren't always looked upon with respect. Many, if not most people have their own opinion of a dreamer: they believe that we're not in touch with reality. On the contrary, we are. We just have the faith in ourselves to back it up.

My opinion is that the "realists" are fearful of the "dreamers" because we dared to believe that there's more to life than living in reality; that, in fact, sometimes our dreams are the very thing we need in order to live our reality. It seems that those with the most opinions are those with the most fear. We become a mirror of who they are, and they don't always like what they see. They see their own fears and restrictions; they realize that their own dreams are lying stagnant because they won't take a chance on catching one. They resent the dreamer for doing what, deep down inside, they'd wish they could… but can't.

What they fail to realize is that they "can!" We all can, yet we have to posses the strength to do it, and not everyone is where the "dreamer" is on their journey. The "realists" have to find their way on their own and face some cold, hard facts about themselves. Deep down inside they're not criticizing us, they're getting angry at themselves. They're wondering how we do it and what is our "secret" to dreaming as big as we do.

There is no secret. There is no method. There is no right or wrong. In this world there are two things: knowing and doing. You have to know who you are in your heart and soul in order to know what you need to get where you want to be.

There's no shame in being a dreamer, nor is there in being a realist. The shame lies within yourself if you allow anyone to make you question who you are. The answer of all that you are and all that you can be is found within you. Only you have the power to change and the strength to do what makes you whole.

"Forget who you were; decide who you are."

"Those That Dare"

As I finish up my time here on the West Coast preparing to go back to the East Coast, I sit and think of the people I've met during this trip. Their stories are very similar, yet the bottom line is this: they dared to take a chance, make a change, and be happy! What a concept that is: dare to be happy!

Most of the stories are about their lives in a place far away, wanting to make a change and only dreaming of it. Yet one day they all woke up and decided to make their move; to leave a life that had done its' time and take a chance to start a new one. Most have moved miles away to do it and left behind friends and family, job security and their own comfort zone. Yet in speaking with them, what they found once they dared to make a change was happiness.

They realized that the move didn't mean they couldn't go back home to visit, or that the friends and family they left behind wouldn't be there. The jobs they had no longer held a sense of purpose for them, so they found jobs they loved somewhere else.

They dared to be happy, took a chance, and found all that they were looking for. It wasn't easy for them, but it was worth it. They heard a lot of negative opinions from some, yet they knew that it was because those that "don't" are afraid of those that "do." Once again, the "realist" fears the "dreamer," because we had the balls, so to speak, to do something that they couldn't, and they couldn't because of their own fears and lack of self-esteem.

Some would rather sit in an unhappy life and play the martyr, seeking the attention of those who will tell them how wonderful they are for staying in the same place or situation. Those that support a martyr are usually ones' themselves. They are just as fearful as the martyr, and they, too, look for validation from other martyrs.

I don't look at martyrs as someone to admire. Some think they should be pitied but I don't. They have the ability to make a choice to live a happy life, yet they choose not to. I have no time for those that "can" but "won't;" for those that would rather complain day after day of all the sacrifices they've made. They made them for a reason; to seek the attention they desire because they're unable to do that for themselves.

ANNE DENNISH

I say this to you: dare to be happy, take a risk, and make a change. It may not always be easy, as we know most things worth having aren't, yet it will be so worth it to you. You'll never know unless you try. The only regret you'll have will always be wondering if you missed an opportunity to find happiness or catch a dream. Dare to be great, dare to be different, dare to be happy!

"The Waiting Game"

There are those who "do" and those who "wait." They wait for us to call, to start or finish a conversation, to give an opinion, share an idea or to tell them how we feel. Those are the ones that are always waiting. Those that "do" are the ones always calling just to say they care or that they are missing someone, the ones who are always saying "I love you" first, the ones always starting the conversation, and the ones' always making those that "wait" feel special.

Yet those that "do" are the ones who need those things more than those that "wait." We're the ones that spend most of our time on those we love, and hope upon hope that someone will be missing us, waiting with baited breath for that next time they hear our voice, starting the conversation and telling us they love us before we have a chance to.

I'm wondering if all relationships are built this way; one person that "does" and one person that "waits." It makes me wonder if these are the relationships that will last, because I know through my own personal growth and experience that if I feel less than what I make someone else feel, that feeling will eventually die... and so will the relationship.

I want to be the "love" of someone's' life, and not simply at the times that suits them, but at the times it suits me. Does it mean that I mean less to the one who waits? Do they love me less? They say actions speak louder than words, and I believe that with all my heart. Words mean nothing unless the action precedes it or follows it immediately after it's said.

"While the words may be all those that you want to hear, it's the actions to back them up that make it truth."

The person who "waits" always feels good about themselves when they're in a relationship with someone who "does." They have an ego that grows with each action they learned to "wait" for. They know how to manipulate the one who "does" by doing nothing when they're given an opportunity of actually doing something. It may sound confusing, yet it's not.

We all want to feel and know love, and most importantly, be shown love. We all want to feel important to someone, and when we don't, the person who "waits" takes it as an attack on who they are; that we're insecure. They seem to lack the ability to understand and the only way they will is if we become the one who waitss and watches what they will "do."

They'll usually do "nothing" and become distant and angry; they may even become vindictive in the smallest of way, showing us who has the upper hand.

What they don't realize is they've begun the process of losing someone that, in fact, they may truly love and who truly loves them back. Yet because of their ignorance and comfort of always having us "do" the emotional thing for them, they're pushing us away. We know in our hearts we've become a matter of convenience, and personally, once I begin to feel that way, all bets are off. I know it's just a matter of time before everything blows, and after that, the end is imminent.

I want the same things I give someone else; I want them to rock my world as I rock theirs'; I want to be missed as much as I miss them and most importantly, I want to be loved as much as I love them.

I don't want to always "do," and I don't want them to always "wait;" I want to feel important and loved, just as I make them feel.

The choice belongs to those who "do" and those who "wait:" don't wait to do what needs to be done.

"The Differences: Embrace Them or Replace Them"

"There are always differences between people; embrace them or replace them."

Siblings, college roommates, spouses, life partners - eventually we'll all be sharing space with someone at one time or another and it isn't until the boxes are moved in and unpacked that you'll see the "differences." Champagne and wine is shared to celebrate this new adventure, and there's a warm, exciting feeling of "this is so great!" Just think, someone to eat with, watch television with, share a beer and some laughs with; it's all so wonderful, isn't it?

It is until someone leaves their dirty dishes in the sink after you cooked the meal, or sits and watches television while you're cleaning the house and doing yard work.

Wow, what the hell happened? Seriously, you don't know? The answer is simple: you moved in with someone who, despite the similarities you shared, is in fact, NOT you, and sharing a space is just another chapter of your life that will bring to light all the differences.

There they are: "the differences!" Welcome to the reality of getting to know someone. It's all fun and games until someone gets hurt or shows their differences.

So what do you do now? This lovely little land of excitement and companionship went from Candy Land to the Game of Life, and you're struggling to win. Yet in life, it's not a game, and shouldn't be a struggle. It's a learning experience of two or more people sharing a space and the lessons will be more about yourself than you would have imagined.

You're a neat freak, they're Pig Pen; they can't sleep with the television on, you can; you take the initiative for housework and yard work, they procrastinate if it can wait until later. You're sweet in the morning, they're sour; they're a night owl, you're a morning glory; you relax after the work is done, they relax before it's even started.

Sounds like a no-win situation, doesn't it? It's not. It's a decision you make based on who you are and perhaps, who you are able to become.

You now know the differences, so ask yourself this: do you want to take the easy way out and replace them, or learn more about how to embrace them?

Every situation is different; every person in it is different, yet why not observe these differences as traits that make life interesting, and in some cases, makes it exciting? Wouldn't it be boring if the other person were exactly like you? Where would the mystery, the challenge, or even the fun be? Personally, I'd be bored if I was with someone "exactly" like me; there'd be nothing new to learn or discover. There'd be no differences to try on and see if they fit.

You can't make someone "be" just like you. Would you really want to? What you can do is discuss the differences and together find the compromise. Sometimes just understanding the differences can be enough to prevent them from being "replaceable." Maybe you can learn to make the differences become "embraceable."

There are no rules that say you can't laugh at the differences, or make fun of them in a non-hurtful way. In fact, laughter IS the best medicine in any situation, and this is no exception. Remember, "first and foremost, find your funny!" This is one of those times it's important to find the funny and release the laughter.

I do, however, caution you NOT to get caught up in the vicious cycle of complaining about the differences all the time, whether it's to that person or other people. The more negative things you say about them, the more negative they become, and that "negative" stuff will become larger than life. If you thought dirty dishes in the sink was annoying, you haven't seen anything yet! The more you complain, the more faults you will find, and the more miserable you will become.

Are dirty dishes and yard work all that important? What about their "heart and soul?" Are they kind, loving, and respectful? Do they care about you and take care OF you? Do they make you laugh? Most importantly: **do they love you?**

If you answered "yes" to just one of those questions, then you may just have to learn to make those differences "embraceable." If you answered "no" then get the moving boxes back out and start packing; you've already decided that they are "replaceable."

You need to look at yourself as well; obviously you chose to share a space with someone you had known for quite some time, and obviously didn't even see the differences in them. In fact, you chose to live with them because you liked who they were, not what they could do. Let's face it, people don't suddenly begin to put dirty dishes in the sink after you've cooked the meal; be honest, they did it all along, but you didn't notice. Now you do.

Ask yourself, is it worth it? Isn't the "heart and soul" of someone much more important than the "cooking and cleaning?" When sharing a space with someone, they are both important issues to work out, but that's just it: it can be worked out. It's much easier to "agree to disagree" than to "disagree to agree."

You can't allow yourself to be the "perfect" person and find fault with someone else, because what you think are great qualities in you, may not be that to them.

"Life is too short and unpredictable to be anything less than happy."

Life is a mindset and you are in control of what you think and feel. You can't blame the differences of another person on making you mad or upset; you allowed it by letting it bother you. Always take the time to look at the situation before you come to any conclusions or decisions; ask yourself if it's worth the trouble and potential argument it may cause.

You must ask yourself how important this person is to you; would you rather live with them and their dirty dishes, or without them but left with a clean sink?

Take those differences and make your decision because the "replaceable can always become embraceable, yet the embraceable can't always be replaceable."

"Be the Doorbell, Not the Doormat"

I'm not one to yell and scream until I'm pushed to the wall. I don't get angry very often, and always try to talk calmly with someone about a situation. I prefer life to be peaceful with as little drama as possible. I avoid stress at all costs. Do you know what those qualities make me to certain types of people? Answer: a doormat.

Yes, sadly to say, there are people who know that they can get away with yelling at me or being verbally abusive because I let them. After years of counseling on such matters, I will still find myself in situations where I'm a doormat, and I hate it. I despise it. It breaks my heart to know that my kind and positive nature is taken advantage of by some people. Yet it still happens and I'm left sitting there, more angry at myself than at them because I allowed them to treat me that way. It's not because I wanted to, it's because I didn't know how NOT to.

Therein lies' my analogy:

A doormat sits on the front porch, and everyone that passes through that door wipes their feet on it. There is no choice for a doormat. It just sits there and takes the abuse. Some will wipe their feet lightly, while some will bury their boots onto it. It's all the same in the end; the difference is the severity of the wiping. Occasionally someone with bare feet will walk upon it, but they're usually filled with sand or mud. No matter the feet, the doormat still sits and takes it, but wait, why be the doormat when you have a choice to be the doorbell?

What's the "doorbell?" Think about it, I've just described the life of a doormat, yet imagine the life of a doorbell?

The doorbell has choices; when someone rings the doorbell, what do you do? Do you immediately rush up to answer the door, or do you, like most of us, peek out the window to see who it is and decide if we want to answer it? Do you realize that in that split second of someone ringing the doorbell you have to decide whether or not to let them come in. There's no thinking about it too long, or giving it a few years to see if you should answer it or not; you have but seconds to make a decision.

That's the difference between a doorbell and a doormat. A doormat can lie there for years until it's worn out and has had enough. No decisions to make quickly, always there to just take what life hands it, no matter what.

WAKING UP

The doorbell has all the advantages and on a timely basis. There's no wasting time to let life hand it what it wants; we make the decision to answer life to what WE want!

So I ask you, as you read this silly analogy of mine, what are you? What are you right at this very moment? Are you living your life as a doormat or are you living it as a doorbell?

If you're a doorbell, good for you! Stay that way!

If you're a door mat, what do you do next? What changes can you make at this very moment to stop lying there and taking all that the "shoes of life" are giving to you on a daily basis? What can you do to start letting life "ring the bell" to give you the power to make a choice?

We all find ourselves feeling like a doormat at one time or another, but it's your choice on how long you lie there. Never feel weak or devalued because you've been taken advantage of now and again. We're all human and we're not meant to be perfect. We are, however, meant to love ourselves to such an extent that no one would be able to treat us like a doormat. They would be honored to "ring our doorbell" and more importantly, they would feel grateful if we answered!

"Down the Explain Drain"

Have you ever noticed how many times in a day you explain yourself? Probably not, because most of us don't realize how we've spent years, if not a lifetime, of explaining ourselves. We're not making "excuses," we're giving "reasons." I never realized just how much I did this until someone pointed it out to me by one simple question:

"Why do you always explain yourself to everyone?"

Once you are made aware of something, you begin to see just how present the "something" really is.

We explain many things: our actions or lack of them, our emotions, thoughts, questions, answers, mistakes, and our shortcomings; the list goes on and on, yet surely you must get the idea. Now, sit back for a moment and think about your day today; how many times did you go down the "explain drain?"

Why do I call it the "explain drain?" It's because it's a drain of your control and intelligence, and of your humility and emotions. You begin explaining yourself to someone and where do all these excuses go? They go into the abyss of "no one cares about your explanations;" they simply wanted to prove to you that they have the upper hand and the control.

Our explanations are the windows of our soul as to who we are. Listen to yourself closely sometime when you are explaining something to someone.

The first thing to do when this situation is upon you is to ask yourself a few questions:

1. Are your explanations "excuses" or "reasons?"

2. Are they warranted and necessary?

   And the most important question, which most of us have no legitimate answer to:

3. Why are you explaining yourself to anyone?????

See, I stopped you, didn't I?

Now that I've made you think for a moment, I'm hoping your next response is:

"Yeah, why AM I explaining anything to anyone?"

And the next and final response, the one that will reveal strength in you that you may not have known you had is this:

"I don't need to explain myself to anyone!"

There you go: you just realized what I had to learn many years ago. You don't owe anyone an explanation unless you choose to give them one.

Repeat this affirmation until you believe it:

> *"I owe myself respect, honesty and truth, and if I truly do that, there is no need to explain anything to anyone. I am in control of my actions and owe no one an explanation for them."*

Once you begin to see the "explain drain," I promise you that you will begin going down it less and less. You may fall short every so often, yet don't be overly concerned about it. You're only human and this is a hard habit to break, especially if you're surrounded by people that ask you questions that I so eloquently call the "make me feel stupid questions." It's those questions for which there truly is NO answer, yet the person that asks it feels the need to control and this is one way to do it.

Here's some examples of the "make me feel stupid questions," which I hope bring a little chuckle to you as you read them. They should make you smile because you've probably been asked them at one time or another.

- "Why did you make this for dinner?"

- "Are you lying to me?"

- "Didn't you see that dirty dish lying there?"

- "Are you okay?"

- "Are you mad at me?"

- "Why is this paper sitting here?"

- "Did you hear me?"

- Why did you do that?"

And my personal favorite: "Are we having fun yet?"

You have to find your funny in life, no matter what that is! So, now that you're aware of "over explaining" or "explaining" at all, let it go and find your funny in their questions that you've felt the need to answer for all these years.

Laugh at the "make me feel stupid questions," learn a good eye roll or gesture to answer them without speaking, and know you still will go down the "explain drain" every so often. If that should happen, remember to do this one thing: "take out the plunger!"

"Caution: Don't Feed The Ego!"

"While you're busy feeding someones' ego, they're busy starving your self-esteem!"

How many times do you find yourself telling someone how wonderful they are? You make it a point to thank them for all the wonderful things they do for you; yet you failed to realize that you deserved the wonderful things as well. You tell them how beautiful or handsome they look; yet you didn't bother to see how beautiful or handsome you look. You tell them how incredibly funny they are, or how sensitive they are; yet you never see those qualities in yourself. You tell them how much you love them and how grateful you are to have them in your life; did they tell you the same?

You are complementing someone and expressing your feelings about them and without a doubt, it builds their self-esteem, right? Wrong! You are feeding their ego, because WE build our own self-esteem. You don't need someone else's validation of who you are to make you believe in yourself and see all the great qualities you possess, yet there are so many of us who believe we do.

Of course it's wonderful to be complemented and told wonderful things about ourselves. Here's the difference between having self-esteem and not: when someone complements you and you say "thank you," then you have self-esteem; if you respond with "really?" then you don't believe that you're worthy of the complement. Do you see the difference? A "thank-you" response tells the other person that you are grateful they noticed what you already know about yourself. When you respond with "really" you leave the door wide open for the other person to take back what they said, or worse yet, you just let them off the hook. At that moment, they realized that you don't value yourself, so why should they?

The moment you say "really" is the moment that certain types of people, especially a narcissist, will realize that they have the control, and that their opinion is what really matters, not yours. Not everyone would take advantage of a "really" personality, yet in my experience, most do. You gave them the control, you handed them the power, and you told them in so many words, "I don't think I'm great, but so glad you do!" In that moment all they are hearing you say is "I don't think I'm great, why should you?"

Here is truth; if you don't think good things about yourself, why should someone else? You don't need validation to know who you are, or how wonderful you are. You want "confirmation" that someone notices the great things about you that you know you are! You want to know that they agree with how you feel about yourself. Do you see the difference now?

You see, while you are constantly telling someone how wonderful they are, and they agree with you, you are feeding their ego, and believe me, that's not something you want to do. The ego responds to life selfishly; self - esteem however, responds to life selflessly! While you're busy feeding their ego, what happens to you? What happens to your self-esteem? It's being starved, because you are spending all your time, energy and words on someone's ego, and they are gaining weight day by day, moment by moment, because of you.

Your self-esteem becomes starved and hungry, and when the moment of discontent occurs, you'll realize that you're dealing with someone who is twice your size in ego, and you are the unmatched opponent in self-esteem. It's simple to know who will win, and it's isn't you. You allowed yourself to be starved of something vital to your existence while you overfed someone who could care less about you.

We don't always recognize that we're doing this until it's too late. This is why it's important that you have the best relationship with yourself first, long before you go into any relationship with someone else. You need to be in love with yourself in order to truly love someone else. You must see and believe all the good things within yourself, because the truth is, you may not get that confirmation from someone else, and truth is, you shouldn't need it at all.

You don't need someone to tell you how great you are; tell yourself that and if someone should confirm what you already know, then be accepting and grateful of the complement they've given you, because you know what? You deserved to hear it! You didn't "need" to hear it; you "deserved" to hear it. There's a difference.

Over inflated egos' don't care what someone else thinks about who they are, they only care about what someone thinks of WHAT they are! Are they good looking? Do they have a great job or a really hot car? Do they have a lot of money that they just want to throw around to impress others with? Yes, that's what the ego wants you to see; the bells and the whistles, which, in the end, will eventually stop ringing and blowing.

The self-esteem wants you to see "within" the person, not "outside" of the person. Are they kind and compassionate? Are they sweet and caring? Do they attract people in a crowd because of their upbeat attitude? That's the music of self-esteem; music that is heard and embraced by those that resonate towards it.

It's simple: ego is about the "outside," while self-esteem is about the "inside." You have a choice: you can feed an ego and starve your self-esteem, OR you can feed your self-esteem and starve an ego. If you believe you're worthy of great things, great things will come to you, and the not so great things will keep their distance.

Life can be like a zoo; ego lives within a cage, just as a dangerous animal does. You're kept out so you don't get hurt. Self-esteem lives on the outside, because there is no danger in feeding oneself. The danger lies within feeding the animals. The choice is yours and yours alone.

My belief is that the best place to view the ego is on the other side of self-esteem.

"I'm Sorry, But I'm Not"

Just as there are habitual liars, there are habitual "apologizers." We all know them, and in some cases, we are them. It's easy to recognize in others because no matter what we say or do, they're always saying "I'm sorry." We can see it in others far easier than in ourselves.

Are you in the habit of saying "I'm sorry?" Listen to yourself when talking to someone else and count the number of times you say it; then take a look at WHY you're saying it so often. It's because it's become a habit, and a bad one at that. We shouldn't apologize to anyone for our feelings. Expressing ourselves is part of loving and respecting ourselves, just as we'd love and respect someone else. Yet so often we've spent much of our lives apologizing.

Don't get me wrong, there are times we need to say "I'm sorry." Accidents happen and we may unintentionally hurt another person's feelings, but please don't apologize for how you feel. The words you choose to express yourself should be done with grace, respect and thought. No one can fault you for how you feel, yet some people do, and that is how we get caught in the habit of always, always, always saying we're sorry.

Perhaps you had a childhood upbringing that believed that "children should be seen and not heard," or were in a relationship that never respected your feelings. The list goes on as to how we got where we are, but let the list stop here! I'm giving you fair warning that you can change the habit of saying "I'm sorry" to the habit of never apologizing for who you are.

We don't always get along with everyone, and that's alright. I don't believe we were put on this Earth to be in relationships with everyone we meet. Remember, it's your feelings that let you choose who you do or don't have in your life, and when someone isn't making you feel good about yourself, be done with them. Don't apologize for feeling uncomfortable in a situation. It's your right and protection of self that makes you feel the way you do.

"Self-protection" is what our inner voice and gut instincts are all about: protecting us from something that doesn't feel right. There's no reason for an apology there.

The habit of apologizing takes control over us and can make us feel small and insecure. The habit of accepting our feelings' gives us control, self-confidence and all the other wonderful things that help to lead us on the path to a great life; a life of loving who we are. There's no apology necessary for that!

Break the habit of "apologizing" today and start tomorrow fresh, with "no apologies" in it!

I'm sorry if this story upsets anyone, yet again, I'm not sorry. I'm choosing to help you along the path to personal freedom, and there's no apology necessary for that!

"Free Will"

Everyone has a choice to make in every facet of their life; it's their "free will." Yet there are times we find that the people closest to us have their own opinion or advice to give us. That's all well and good, should we ask for it. They are usually the people who love and care for us the most; the ones who don't want to see us get hurt by making a mistake or bad decision.

Yet when you "tell" someone how to handle something in their life you have just interfered with their free will, disallowing them their choice to make a mistake or bad decision. After all, those mistakes and decisions are ours, and ours alone; they are the ones that become our teacher as to why we made them in the first place; they are our lessons to learn. So, it's not too difficult to understand that, while we can stand by someone, even though we believe that they're making a mistake, we must love them enough to allow them to make it. It's their life, their journey, and if we somehow thwart the choice that life has given them, we are the ones that actually hurt them more than the mistake.

Loving someone is powerful, whether it's your child, friend, or life partner. Of course we don't want to see them fall or be hurt because our love for them allows us to feel their pain as well. Yet our role should be to allow them the freedom to make their choices, whether or not we believe them to be the right ones. Should they make the wrong decision, our role is to stand by them, not in front of them; to love them through it. It's not our role to take away their free will by intervening in a situation that life was handing them in order to teach them something about themselves.

Do you see the difference? I learned it the hard way. All the while I was thinking I was helping someone, I was hindering their growth. That pertains to our children as well. Of course, when they're younger, we do have to make some decisions for them, because they're simply not mature enough to understand certain things. Yet as they grow older, we have to let them make a mistake or two, as long as it's one that's not life threatening.

I can remember a few times when my children were teenagers when they actually got angry at me for allowing them to do something that I knew they'd get in trouble for. They would ask me why I let them do it. My answer was always "so you could learn a lesson; did you learn one?" Their answer was usually: "yeah, to never to do it again." There you go, I didn't mess with their free will, they made a mistake, yet they learned not to do it again. More importantly, they learned WHY they shouldn't have done it at all.

Love those in your life enough to let them make their own choices, because when you take away their "free will" to do that, you're also taking away their freedom. We try to protect those we love, yet sometimes the greatest protection is the first mistake we allow them to make; it may be the time they'll learn never to do it again.

"The Discomfort Zone"

"Sometimes we have to do something uncomfortable in order to become comfortable."

I once had to make a decision I never wanted to make, and the reality is, there have been a few times I had to do that. It was a decision that was in my best interest and more importantly, the best interest of my children (which always makes it harder when it's for them!) It's a decision that would allow us to do something that we hadn't done with ease for quite some time: "breathe."

As a single mother of five, life has been a bit difficult financially. I lived the life of a millionaire for many years during my first marriage. I found myself "comfortable" after the divorce, only to find myself nearly destitute from the second marriage. Yet, I'm a mom that believes that as long as you hold onto your faith strongly and keep fear away, everything will work out; and it has. No, I do not have millions, not even close, but just when the bottom was mere inches from hitting, an Angel dropped in…in many forms and in many ways.

It was the most valuable lesson I could teach and share with my children: stay strong, stay positive and keep the faith. My mantra to them became: "it won't be like this forever, just for today."

So, when breast cancer hit, it was no different. I sat with my three boys who still lived home and told them I had cancer. Three sets of eyes began to tear up, three sweet mouths opened slightly, yet there was no sound of those precious voices; not a word, not a laugh or giggle, not even a cry. I will forever remember the look of fear that crossed a 12, 16, and 19 year old boys face.

Yet I wouldn't let them be afraid, because I wasn't. My biggest "concern" was losing my hair and not knowing if chemo would render me unable to function, sick to my stomach, bed ridden, or worse, looking like a mere skeleton of the mother they knew. Yet there was no time for concerns, this was time for action. Start treatment immediately and get this party started (because this was truly a party I didn't want to stay at long!)

I was fine after my first chemo. I had just had a port surgically implanted into my chest in the morning and my first round of chemo in the afternoon. I came home to my kids, who were standing looking at me. "Now what?" one of them asked me. "Should you lie down or something?"

WAKING UP

I thought about it, and chose "something!" I started dinner, went on the computer, spent some time with my kids and went to bed. The "something" I chose was "normal."

And then I went back to work. Chemo on Thursday filled with drugs and steroids, which would give me bright red cheeks throughout my morning on Fridays, along with an appetite to choke a horse! The red cheeks faded to a normal color by Friday afternoon, and the appetite went back to normal...somewhat normal. I realized that there would be no worries of weight loss from chemo for me!

I lost my hair and found a short version of it in a sassy, sexy little wig. Short version? I loved the wig, and if you have to lose your hair, you might as well look amazing until it grows back! It was sexy, sassy and ME! "She" and I fell in love instantly. "She" made my life as easy as it could be; no blow dryers, gels, mousse or hair spray; just shake it out, put it on, adjust, brush and go! "She" kept our secret well, as most people didn't know it was a wig unless I told them. It was a match made in heaven and a fair trade-off: I would have rather had no hair and a great wig than to have had cancer and refused treatment because of the side effects.

Life is filled with many discomfort zones, and they're not all as serious as cancer. Throughout my cancer, which you would think was my biggest "discomfort zone," I went through a break-up and some financial worries. The break up was harder than the cancer, mainly because you know your odds with cancer, not so much with relationships! Matters of the heart are more of a crap shoot than the "standard procedures" of breast cancer.

I had to make some uncomfortable decisions about my finances, which as difficult as the process was, I turned my "discomfort zone" into one that was most definitely more comfortable. The process was not one was I had planned for in my life, yet sometimes the unexpected of plans rewards us with some pretty great surprises.

As far as the break up, well, let's just say, not all men are meant to stay in your life, and that goes for women too. People come into our life for a reason, and are meant to stay for a certain amount of time, be it a few months, years, or a lifetime. We learn a lot about ourselves through other people; everyone you meet is a mirror to your soul, and we see ourselves differently in each one. You just need to be smart enough to know that those mirrors you see less of yourself in are not the ones meant to be in your life for too long.

You see, with the right mindset you can turn your "discomfort" zone into your "comfort" zone. It may not be exactly how you wanted it, but remember what I told my kids: "it won't be like this forever, just for today."

"Don't Shoot Your I Out"

The way we speak and phrase our thoughts is important. The way we perceive ourselves through language is imperative. What you say is what someone else hears, and from that one sentence or phrase, they begin to have an understanding of who you are.

I've had many teachers throughout my life, read many books on enlightenment and relationships, and observed many different people through many scenarios. The one important thing I've learned is this: never lose your "I." The moment you do, you're blind, and what others see is an easy target, and in some instances, a victim who has no value to themselves, only to those around them.

How often do you shoot your "I" out? Listen to yourself closely for just one day, and you'll be shocked at how often you say "we, us, they or ours." You know what that says about you? That you don't know how to exist as just yourself; that you need someone or many someone's in your life to validate you as a person. When you've lost the "I" in speaking, you've lost yourself in living.

Need an example? I have a friend who is going through a divorce. She asked me for advice along the way, knowing that I had gone through it myself. I remember telling her that it may be the ending to a marriage, but it was the beginning of a new life for her; it was the beginning of her having a life of her own. I explained the importance of not losing herself again, as she had in her marriage. She became excited at the prospect of making her life her own and hopeful at all the possibilities she would soon have. She became confident, or so I thought.

What happened next? That's easy: she fell in the love with the first man she met. She wasn't divorced yet, hadn't redone the house, or found out anything about herself as a single woman or who she really was outside of a relationship. She raced into his arms and began speaking a language that drove me absolutely crazy! Every single sentence she spoke to me began with "we, our, or he." You get the idea; not one sentence was ever about her and her alone. I spoke to her about this and thought she understand what I was saying. She was no longer the good friend I thought she was, but worse than that, she had been on the brink of finding herself until she lost herself in him. She threw herself head on into the relationship and became a foreign person to me. She lost the ability to talk about anything or anyone else other than him. I no longer wanted to be involved in a friendship with a woman that turned into a friendship with this man. She lost her

"I," and she lost her friend, yet she didn't seem to care. She was in love and to those who don't value themselves in the first place, it's inevitable that this will happen.

Losing her "I" made her lose her perspective on her life. She was too scared to live a life alone long enough to find out who she really was or is. Losing your "I" makes you blind to everyone and everything around you, except the reason you lost your "I" for in the first place.

It's not always another person that makes you lose your "I." It could be a job, a career, or even a group of friends, yet I've learned that nothing and no one is worth losing your "I" over. No one who respects you would want you to lose your "I" unless of course they want to control you and the situation, which so often is usually the case. This brings me back to my original statement: if you don't value yourself enough to begin with, no one else will, and you will attract people and situations that are more than willing and happy to take your "I" from you. You're blind and can't see it, but they can, and they will present themselves as a bright light, the answer to your prayers, the end all to be all, because they know you have no idea who you are, so they'll make you who they want you to be.

There's always a way to regain your "I" when it's been lost, yet it usually happens through loss, heartache and sometimes, through financial ruin. It's through those things that we finally see that we gave our "I" away willingly; we just didn't realize at the time that we were actually doing that.

"Hindsight is the ability to see in the present what we were unable to see in the past."

Hindsight is truth, and we must understand that we are in control of our own life, thoughts, and actions, and if we give that power over to someone else then most assuredly it will not end well.

"If you don't value yourself, how will anyone else see value in you?"

You have to know yourself and your worth. Only you can love yourself into a beautiful "I" to stay safe from those that will take it away. Remember, you gave away your "I" willingly once, and you are the only one to get it back!

I no longer talk to my friend and that was my choice. She was no longer anyone I knew; she morphed into him and his life, and that's not who I was friends with. I wish her well, yet I know where time will take her. The friendship was foreign to me, yet I began to see her differently. The reality is that the person I thought she was never really existed. The sadness is that she never knew who she was, and she never will at this point.

Don't shoot your "I" out, and don't be afraid of not knowing if you've become blind or not. Love and respect yourself; these are but some of the safety tools that will prevent that from happening to you. If you can do all of those things for yourself, you'll never be in danger of "shooting your *I* out!" On the contrary, you will be in a position to attract the right people and situations that will love, respect and embrace your "I."

I was taught a few years ago by a very smart lady, that there are three parts to a good relationship, no matter what type it is: them, you, and us. It's two people who each have their own life, their own "I" and bring it together for a well rounded and healthy "us."

No good "us" is born from the lack of an "I." The perfect "us" comes from a valuable "you" and a valuable "them." The rest falls into place.

Protect your "I," wear safety goggles of respect and love for yourself, and I promise you this: you'll never have to worry about someone "shooting your "I" out again!"

"The True Colors of Relationships"

There exists a "sadness" when your world explodes; when everything and everyone you believed to be a certain way turns out to be completely different. This realization rocks your world, breaks your heart, and dispels all truths you believed in the first place. There isn't anything more shattering than being a believer that "there is good in everyone," only to find out that this is not always true; that those of us who try to live as a respectful, loving, compassionate human beings must one day come face to face with someone who is the opposite, someone who we saw all the good in, only to find out it wasn't truth at all. The truth was in finding out who they were, what they are, and what they have to gain. Truth and lies hurt, yet the deception of what and who we perceive to be real is the worst sadness of all. We believed in someone or something, only to be shown that believing isn't enough; it's actually the "seeing" and the "feeling" that is the believing. Hold on to your hats when this happens because once you enter this type of storm, all bets are off, and you find yourself staring into the belly of the beast; you will inevitably be the one hurt as you're left in ruins as they run free. Just as they brought you the ultimate sadness, they will bring it to others as well because it's all that they know and that's called "soul-less."

I sometimes wonder whether we suffer a broken heart or hurt feelings because someone treated us badly, or is the reason for those feelings because what we had believed all along to be true simply wasn't.

There are times that each and every one of us begins to think about someone in our past. Truth be told, we do this to get through the pain. We hold on to the great times and memories we had with them, only because it's too painful to remember the pain they caused us. This happens all too often in relationships. When one person hurts you, someone else who had hurt you before them looks better, and that's where we have to be very careful NOT to go back in time, to realize that "sometimes we have to revisit the past to remember why we left it in the first place." It's all too easy to do this, and is not something to feel badly about. Life is a matter of survival, and a broken heart is no different. We do what we have to do to get through it. Trust me, thinking of an ex-friend, lover, or partner when someone else causes us pain is nothing more than false feelings, and is, after all, nothing more than a "fantasy" to block the pain. You'd be better off reading Cinderella than to go back to an old relationship of any type.

"Sometimes we have to revisit the past to remember why we left it there in the first place."

The same is true where friendships are concerned. We all find ourselves in the perfect camaraderie with someone at one time or another. It's a relationship that lasts a short time or in some cases, a long time. We somehow believe that a friendship that lasts for years is meant to last a lifetime, yet this isn't always true. You have to remember one very important factor: people change with time and circumstance. Friendships are no different. Some of them survive the changes with time, while others may not. Some people simply grow up and away from a friendship that once served them; one that served both parties. Yet, as time goes on, what once was a close bond of friendship is found strained, until the point when the bonds are broken, as well as the people involved.

I'll admit that some end a friendship easily; they move on as they move up in their life. As new people drop into their world, we no longer find ourselves part of it. The head accepts that friendships may grow apart and even end, yet the heart takes much more time to accept that. After all, the heart is where the emotions and the feelings are; the head is where logic lives.

And life is not always logical.

One party is usually much more injured than the other; it's usually the friend that moved on that does so with ease and lack of remorse. The other friend is hurt and disappointed. That's the way life goes; most relationships of any kind that end are usually ended by one, and the other is left with no choice other than to accept their decision. We don't like it and we feel as though we had no say in the matter, yet when someone decides to move on, the friendship or relationship is done.

We're left injured and angry; we're left shocked and surprised. We thought that communication would solve the problem, and that while we could accept a change in the friendship, we wouldn't accept the end of it. Circumstance plays a large role in all of this; friends change in our eyes because true colors are revealed through circumstance. We see the colors, and it isn't the colors of a rainbow. We definitely don't want to see the truth, and the truth is that all the qualities you once shared in the friendship are suddenly gone; someone lost the loyalty, someone lost sight of the big picture, and someone lost sight of "you." That is why we feel hurt. We give them the benefit of the doubt, intuitively knowing that they've betrayed the loyalty of the friendship, yet still hoping the rainbow will surface, and they will see that they were wrong to treat us that way. You're a bit shocked that they couldn't do what you would have liked, which is to be loyal, yet not surprised because the signs were there all along, and as humans we sometimes choose not to see them.

WAKING UP

We are all responsible for our actions in every facet of our lives; we are NOT responsible for the actions of another. It's normal to feel hurt and betrayed, because in many cases, that's what their actions made you feel. It's normal to still wish it could all go back to the way it was, yet it won't. It's normal to sit and think of all the time of your life you've spent with them and wonder how they could throw something away so easily, yet they don't care. Therein lies the hurt; you cared, they didn't. Therein lies the anger; you were loyal, they weren't.

So what are you left with? The lessons of what you learned, the acknowledgment of the signs you ignored, and once again, the realization that until you love and respect yourself as you should, no one else will either.

Sit and think about what ended and how you're feeling; feel all of that and then let it all go. Sit and think of how your life changed since they left. Are you in a better place? Are you happy? Did new friends find you? Most of you will answer "yes" and then wonder why you've spent any amount of time on the friend that left. You spent that time in order to heal; to accept who they've become; and to understand that maybe they were that way all along. Perhaps YOU needed them more than they needed you; perhaps YOU made them into the friend you thought they were; perhaps YOU grew as a person along the way, and YOU brought out the fear in them. You made them have to face themselves, and if they weren't able to face their own true colors, they walked away from it all.

Friends should be a rainbow of colors, with a pot of gold at the end for both of you. When the rainbow fades, the pot of gold disappears. We're all human, and we all have a choice to be the best of who we can, yet we must accept and understand that not everyone is in that place in their life journey. They may be stuck in the storm, no rainbow in sight, yet you can move past it and allow the true colors of a rainbow of friends to shine above and around you.

Life changes, friends come and go, yet true love of self is the only way to surround yourself with the ones' that will stay. Find your true colors, and you'll be able to see someone elses' as well.

ANNE DENNISH

"Life After Life After Life"

I've been going to the same hair salon for over twenty years, so needless to say, they know me well. They've known me through three of my five pregnancies, two divorces, and a bad relationship or two. They've watched me struggle with my children as a single mom, watched an anxiety level larger than Mt. Rushmore surface at times, and seen me fall from grace more times than I can count, yet they've also seen me at peace; they've seen me happy.

Which brings me to my question: is there reason to miss the life before the life we're currently in?

I view life as a book. Each chapter is the next part of our life, and as most sayings go, you can't move forward if you keep reading the same chapter. You'll never know where the book of your life is going, and when we read a book, especially if it's a good one, don't you want to know how it ends? Don't you get excited to get to the next chapter to see what happens next?

I've met people who say "I miss my old life." Why? Why would you miss something you left that brought you to something better? Their answer is that they usually miss something they used to do that was fun to them, which in essence, was their passion.

So what's the difference between missing your passion and missing your old life? Your passion is something you love, all your own, that you can carry from life to life. Missing your old life is not finding what you were looking for in your new life. It's important to remember that you left the old life for a reason and in most instances the reason is the same: it wasn't working out. It lost its sparkle, lost its shine, and more importantly, it lost the love. Whether it was love for a significant other, a friend, or job, the love went away, and the shine it once held was dulled. Why in the world would you miss that? The new life you enter should be one of bells and whistles, excitement, newness, and of course, sparkle and shine. The new life may last a lifetime, each chapter becoming more and more exciting, as well it should be, and if it doesn't last, it was still worth moving onto the next part of the book.

Your passion is all your own; it can be shared with someone, yet it exists because of you and who you are. It will always be a part of your old life, because passions never burn out, unless you allow them to. You carry your passion throughout each life you live, sharing it with those you allow, yet when the old life is done, you can still carry that passion with you. After all, it's a part of who you are, and while it may change in time or disappear altogether, it's ultimately your decision. You decide the life of your passion, and yes, sometimes the passion will burn out as time goes on; and sometimes it won't. Yet know to your toes that it is that piece of you that you choose to carry from chapter to chapter.

Be aware of the difference between missing your old life and missing your passion. An old life that wasn't working should never be missed, because it allowed a better life to come in. A passion is only missed if you allowed it to burn out. Share your passion with whomever you'd like but never share that old life with the new; remember that you left it in the first place for a reason.

"The Mind of a Heart"

Sometimes, out of the blue, something wonderful happens. It's nothing you were looking for or thought you even wanted, yet there it is, right in front of you; it's a grand adventure! I've learned a thing or two in this life of mine so far, and that is this: that everything happens for a reason, happens as it should, and happens when it should. It's at that moment you realize that no matter how "in control" of your life you may think you are, the heart has a mind of its' own, and truth be told, many times the heart is smarter than the mind at the exact moment it needs to be.

We spend too much time thinking, planning, arranging and deciding what we do and don't want in life that we often forget that the heart may know better. It's at that single moment that the heart takes us where we need to be, and if we can simply let go of the fear, all will happen as it should, with little or no pain, heartache, or problems.

Fear stops us from so many wonderful things. If we could just throw caution to the wind and trust, we'd realize that an amazing amount of abundance and joy will follow. It took me years to learn how to release my fears about anything and everything, yet once I did so many wonderful things fell into my life, and they fell at the very moment that my heart knew they needed to. It was the exact moment that this "your life is written when you're born" belief decided it should happen.

Fear is a thing of the past for me, although I will admit, there are times I let it get the best of me. Yet when that happens I know what I need to do. Sit quietly alone, outside in the sun or under the stars, and listen to my intuition… listen to my heart. Within minutes all fear is gone, and that feeling of peace and happiness reappears; that moment of "trust" comes rushing back in. I have to say, it's one of those moments in my life that I love.

Fear can stop some truly, amazing things from happening to us and it can prevent us from moving forward from an old chapter of our life into a new, more exciting one filled with all good things. Fear holds us back, holds us down, and holds us under. We have the choice to allow it to do that, or smack it in the proverbial face, release it, and "go with the flow" of what life has to offer. We may not know the outcome, yet isn't it far worse to feel afraid rather than take a leap of faith to see what life holds for us? Isn't it worth the chance to discover what our "heart" knows we need?

ANNE DENNISH

Take a chance and wake up tomorrow morning with no fear. Try waking up with complete acceptance and allowance to let life take you where it knows you need to go. Don't miss out on a grand adventure because fear said you couldn't have one. You have a choice to make your own decisions, and when the heart decides to take control of the mind, your adventure is about to begin!

"What is Love?"

A friend of mine is going through a tough time in her marriage, so for some unknown reason, she's asking me for advice. I listened, I supported, I encouraged, but what she asked me next threw my mind into a tail spin! For the first time, I had no answer and have truly been thinking about how to answer this question:

"What is love?"

I'm a Pisces, so you would think the answer would have come easily, yet I'm no expert. I thought I was in love so deeply two times that I married them both, and divorced them both. I can tell you honestly that both times I truly believed I was in love, yet the funny thing is that love felt different each time. The first marriage happened when I was 25 years old, young enough to be filled with dreams of the perfect life. After 20 years we realized we were far from perfect and the love we thought we had? Well, that had dwindled long before the marriage ended. The second marriage happened when I believed I was older and wiser, yet your mid 40's isn't exactly old either. This love felt different. It felt more mature and I thought was the kind that would last a lifetime. The lifetime of that love lasted only 2 years, when suddenly I realized that the person I had fallen in love with was simply the person who he believed I wanted. Once the ring was on my finger, the real man stepped in, and the love stepped out of my heart and onto a divorce decree.

So, here I sit, wondering how to answer my friend. What I thought was love never really was…or was it? Is love different with every person you "fall in love" with? Does it depend on your age, or situation, or what you want in life? Do we "fall in love" to morph into the person we want to be or to have the life we think we want?

Do we really, CAN we really, fall in love with another person so deeply that it will last a lifetime? Is there a love that will last through the good and bad, the richer or poorer, and more importantly, the better or worse? Or do we simply and unintentionally "fall in love"…with love?

I'll spend the rest of my life believing in love, otherwise I'll lose hope that maybe, just maybe, I'll meet someone that will show me what love is. Actually, let me rephrase that: maybe I'll meet someone that TOGETHER we'll discover what love is. Hmmm, maybe that's a key phrase in what could be the answer to "what is love?" Perhaps love is an emotion we feel by "falling in love" together;

a love that grows through a deep friendship, trust, respect, and most importantly, through laughter.

Love requires two people who are willing and able to fall in love together, and if you ask me if I believe in love at first sight, I would tell you "no." I believe in "excitement" at first sight, a connection, and a physical attraction, but love at first sight? Absolutely not, and I can say that because I've experienced it twice before and know where it ended both times. I believe that you can love someone you enjoy being with, but the real excitement begins as you spend more and more time together, build a relationship of friendship and trust, and fall in this "love" together.

I used to say that I was a "hopeless" romantic, but as I've gotten older I've realized that I am a "hopeful" romantic. I believe in love and all the magic that comes with it, and hope that sometime before my life is over I will experience the real thing: true love in its purest, most innocent, wonderful form. I have to believe that to be true. I'm not looking for love, nor am I waiting for it to find me. There's too much else in life to be experiencing. Love shouldn't feel like a job we're looking for; it should be that "crazy thing" that happens to us when we least expect it. Think about it, wouldn't you rather have a surprise party than a planned party where you know the guest list, the menu and the DJ? I know I would! I believe that the best love is the one that surprises us when we least expect it, not one that we had to look for.

Foreigner sang it best in their song lyrics: "I want to know what love is, I want you to show me." I can tell you I had five people show me true love, and that was my children. I was shown true love when I fell in love with each of them on the day they were born. Five babies showed me true love when two husbands couldn't. They taught me that love isn't selfish or egotistical; it has no boundaries or limitations; it can be heartbreaking and wonderful at the same time, exciting and mundane all at once, yet one thing it taught me is this: love can last forever.

So, in answer to my friends' question: "what is love?" I don't know quite how to answer that just yet. What I do know is that when I'm lucky enough to find it, you'll be the first one I call to tell you the answer. Maybe the answer isn't about knowing *what* it is, but knowing *when* it finds you.

"The Ghosts of Relationships Past"

"At one time or another we have to revisit our past if only to remember why we left if there to begin with."

The past is the past is the past, yet it's our past that brought us to our present, which enables us to manifest our future. Sound complicated? It's not.

Every experience and relationship that has happened to us throughout our life journey has brought us to "now." While it's healthy to move on from the past, it's important to take only with us what we learned, and that can be the complicated part, especially when the "heart" is involved. Broken hearts take time to heal, and we tend to forget about understanding the lessons until the heart feels better. It's valuable time wasted while we're waiting for the heart to catch up to what the mind already knows, yet it's sometimes unavoidable and in many instances, it's a necessary part of the process.

When you leave a job, or a job leaves you, you take with you what experiences you gained, whether it was computer skills, bookkeeping, or learning a new business. You miss it for a day or two and then move on to the next job, which is usually a better one that pays more money and makes you happier.

Relationships are very similar, until the heart is involved. Boyfriend, girlfriend, husband, wife, friend; they're all the same. Hearts are involved and hearts are broken. The level of brokenness depends on the type of role you played in the relationship, which in turn, determines the healing process.

Yet don't be fooled into thinking that you won't survive, or the heart will always stay broken, because that's not true. You actually have the control and the power to allow it to heal at your pace, not theirs.

"A broken heart is proof that it still works."

Yes it is proof. If you weren't able to love, your heart would never be able to be hurt, and that's step one in the healing process: to accept that your heart works.

The next step is to revisit the past; go back to the relationship with clear eyes, wounded heart and all, and honestly look at what had ended. Ask yourself this: "Had the relationship ever really begun?"

ANNE DENNISH

"Sometimes what we think is ending never had a beginning at all."

When we look at our past clearly and objectively, we most always see our part in the demise of it. After all, it takes two to begin something, and two to end it, even if you think you played a role in it or not. It's a wonderful moment of "waking up" when you can see things for what they truly are, and take your own accountability for your role in it. There are times we reconcile or go back with that person for a brief time, if only to realize why we left there in the first place. It doesn't matter what your method of revisiting your past is, just know that there are times you must do it in order for your heart to heal.

Once you've done that, go back to the very place your heart was broken. It's time to go looking for the pieces so that you can put it back together. It's an important part of the healing process to remember the broken heart scenario. Face your fears, face your demons, and go reclaim that space which someone tainted for you. Don't lose a "happy place" because someone hurt your heart there. Take all that you learned from the relationship, including your role in the demise that you figured out, and go pick up the pieces of your heart.

Now, begin to put the pieces back together. Understand that you may not find all of them, and they may not fit together the same as before your heart broke, but you'll find they fit together better. They're stronger and less likely to break as easily as they did the first time.

Now you know why you had to revisit your past to know why you left it behind; it's because you've learned things about yourself you never knew, and it's what you've learned that will make you stronger. You gained insight, wisdom, and strength, and it's the combination of all those things that will put those broken heart pieces right back into place.

Broken hearts are necessary. No one knows for sure why they happen, but I've come to believe they happen for a reason: to teach us about ourselves, to let us know that we may have been settling for something less than what we deserved, or just to let us know we were able to love again, and again, and again!

"A State of Affairs"

Have you ever found yourself straying from your marriage or relationship only to find yourself tangled in a state of affairs? It all seems so exciting and fulfilling at first, yet it's one of the loneliest places you'll find yourself living in. It's one filled with definitive rules, perfect timing, and "the other person." You know, that "other person" who is oblivious to what's going on around them and under their nose; the "innocent" party in the relationship who's going through life with blinders on. They don't know what's going on around them, and you have to be ever so careful, because sooner or later, that oblivious state they live in will blow wide open and blindside them!

Once you're found out, YOU will be the one to be blindsided even more when you see a side of them you never thought existed.

I'm not judging anyone living in a "state of affairs" because those of us who stray have reasons for doing so. Yet, I will tell you that living in one seems exciting at first, filling voids of the heart we never knew we had. It all feels so good that you really trick yourself into believing it's the best thing you could do for yourself. The lies have become your best kept secret… until the secret is found out.

Before long that "state" you live in begins to feel different; you don't like having certain hours to call or meet; you start to need them and want them more, and it begins to get more difficult to sneak around. In fact, this "state" that filled the voids of your relationship is now beginning to have voids of its' own. The "state" that began simply as harmless fun and excitement that you needed to get through a day will suddenly take an ugly turn, and you become ugly right along with it.

The "happy" feeling you once had starts to feel "sad" because you begin to miss them. You can't call every time you feel like it; you have to hide text messages, find pseudo names on line, and the list goes on. With all that deception and hiding, can this "state of affairs" be right?

> *"The best relationship is the one that brings out the best in you, and never hurts anyone you love."*

Sound a bit harsh? It's not meant to; it's meant to make you think. I know of all those feelings and of the emptiness which goes along with it. I know the pain of making a mistake and of never being able to go back once it's made. I know, I understand, and I'd be the first to say "think before you blink...twice if you have to!"

Let's face facts: marriages and relationships don't end because of an affair. An affair is merely a symptom of a broken relationship. There were already problems to begin with, and honestly, sometimes we don't realize how bad the problems are until we cross over to the "state of affairs." It takes two to break a relationship, yet it can take only one to blow it out of the water.

The fact is simple: no one enters a "state of affairs" if their marriage and relationship are healthy and strong, with both people happy. They enter it out of a loss of emotion and feelings of an empty heart; yet they also enter it because they've changed into someone they're not. On the other hand, they might just need to change and don't want to because of their fear of the unknown.

Remember when our parents used to say "it's all fun and games until someone gets hurt?" That rings true with an affair. It is all fun and games. It becomes filled with excitement over doing something you know you shouldn't and knowing that you're getting away with it. Think about it this way: an adult having an affair is no different than a teenager acting out as a rebel behind their parents' back. Drag racing, drinking, doing things our parents told us not to do was exciting... as long as we were getting away with it. Yet how did we feel when they found out?

Party crashers! Suddenly, all that fun stopped dead in its' tracks, and we most certainly suffered the ramifications of our parents wrath from lying to them! While they were only telling us what to do to keep us safe, we blatantly behaved in a way that told them we didn't want to be safe and didn't want to do what they said! Our parents loved us and wanted to take care of us, yet we blindsided them when we got caught; and we paid a price.

"The truth is free; lies will cost you a price."

A lie is a lie, deception is deception, and once you break the trust you have with someone, it's broken for a long time, and from my experience, doesn't always mend back to its' original state. It heals much differently, which affects everyone concerned.

"Everything can be forgiven, yet not everything can be repaired."

Our parents' caught us breaking the rules, yet more importantly, they caught us breaking their trust. We got punished and with that, they became the private detectives of our every move, simply because we broke the trust.

My belief is this: "state of affairs" happen because we're not whole; we're hurting and we're missing something. What you have to realize is that YOU have to fill the void, YOU have to figure out what you are missing, and YOU need to understand why you are hurting. Someone on the outside can fill the emptiness temporarily, whether it be through having an affair or simply by how you choose to live your life. No one can fill your emptiness, or love you and be your happiness; you have to do that all on your own. I can promise you this, until YOU do it all for YOU, no one else can or will either. It's a temporary fix that can cause a lifetime of broken pieces.

"If you're not willing to love yourself unconditionally, why would you expect anyone else to do it for you?"

And that is the "state of affairs;" you don't love yourself enough, so you throw caution to the wind and logic out the window. You go for the easy way out by letting someone else try and fix your broken pieces.

Sorry to say, it's never going to work… no way, no how, not ever!

Love yourself first, and above all else, be kind to yourself. We all make mistakes, and some of us may currently be in a "state of affairs." Change it before it changes you; leave it before it leaves you; and love yourself, because it doesn't love you in the way you deserve. Until you love yourself the way you want to be loved, it won't ever happen.

If you're in a state of affairs now, you can get out, and hopefully with minimal damage. If you're in for the long haul, get out of the short haul. But whatever your choice, do it while your mind is in the right place.

"It takes but one moment of ignorance to cost you a lifetime of bliss."

We're human and we make mistakes, and that's perfectly normal as long as we learn the lessons from them.

If you're in a "state of affairs" take a minute and think about why. Affairs aren't always about them or us or we; they're about "you."

Don't settle for less than you deserve; reach for the stars. Your "state of affairs" may be your star and if that's true, you need to leave what was once your "moon" to be in it.

ANNE DENNISH

Do what needs to be done for YOU, because the best YOU help's to make the best of those around you. Don't get sucked into a "state of affairs" to fill a void; expand yourself into a "state of affairs" with yourself; you may just find that the moon and the stars were within you all along!

"Sometimes We Go Back"

Relationships come and go; they last for a brief time or a life time. Yet when they end, do they really end? Are all ties cut? Do you move on as if nothing happened? Some may move on quickly, while others' may not.

Our heart tells us to move forward, yet sometimes we go back; and sometimes going back is the best thing we could possibly do.

We've all been there and done that at least once; we leave a relationship or a marriage and during that period of time we're apart from who we thought was "the one," we grieve, we feel lonely, and we feel lost. Some of us even feel stuck. What do we do with these emotions and those feelings of not being able to move on? What then?

It takes but one phone call, instant message or text from the one that left us to make us re-think our own moving forward. Suddenly, this relationship that we knew was destined for destruction looks somehow completely different; in fact, it looks wonderful! Our hearts can trick our mind into thinking that the "not so nice" person who stole our self-esteem and self-respect suddenly looks like the best thing that ever happened to us. Isn't that right?

Wrong! It's very wrong, yet until you "go back" you won't see that. Thus my reasoning for the fact that sometimes we MUST go back to remember why we left in the first place, because in the end, it will be the greatest lesson we learn for ourselves!

I'm not suggesting that everyone should reconcile with every single person from each relationship that ended; you intuitively know which relationship to go back to. Sometimes you'll go back to every one of them, but the key is that you don't stay too long or go back permanently. You go back to finish something that wasn't finished, but you must understand that it was finished for them, just maybe not for you. You need to go back to pick up the pieces of yourself that they chipped away at. You need to find out how to repair the damage. You need to get your self-esteem and self respect back on board. And sometimes the way we do that is to go back, because the reality is that when someone has hurt you that badly, the "going back" is never the same. You know in your heart it will never work, but it's similar to having an injury that won't heal quickly…it takes time.

My own personal experience of "going back" didn't mend or fix an already broken relationship, but instead taught me lessons about myself. I learned more about my strengths and weaknesses, what made me feel high and low, and what questions to ask of myself, the most important one being: do you love yourself? Next question: how much?

If you don't love yourself with complete abandon, no one else will either. How can you expect the "one" to love you if you can't be "the one" to love yourself?

We all tend to have a ready list of our faults and shortcomings, and are still trying to write the list of our strengths and great qualities. So in the midst of not having the good list written, we meet someone. They're wonderful, perfect, and we believe them to be "the one." And sometimes they are... for awhile. Suddenly that perfect person isn't treating you so perfectly, and is starting to complain and pick at things about you. You feel hurt, and let's face it, shocked that anything about you was suddenly bothering them. Think about why this happened: YOU DIDN'T WRITE THE GOOD LIST ABOUT YOURSELF BEFORE ENTERING THE RELATIONSHIP!!!!

You see, that "good list" about yourself should be first and foremost before entering any relationship, because without it, you forget it. And you forget because you never reminded yourself of your good qualities.

So, the relationship ends because the other person only saw your "not so good" list, and you're the only one to blame, yet until you realize that you played a part in this, you go back...and so you should!

Go back and find your good list, go back with your eyes wide open and the rose colored glasses thrown in the garbage! Go back like a virgin and look at it as if it IS your first time! I bet it looks a lot different, and it looks different because the experience of that break up made you different; it forced you to look at yourself differently, and that is why you had to go back... to remember.

"Why Wasn't I Good Enough"

There's a scene in the movie "When Harry Met Sally" in which Sally is crying to her friend, Harry, about her ex-boyfriend who asked someone to marry him only a short time after he broke up with her. She was hysterically crying because he had told her he never wanted to get married and she had spent years with him. Now, suddenly he wants to get married…just not to her.

Movies can sometimes be as true as life, which is why someone wrote the screenplay in the first place; personal experience. I'm sure everyone has gone through their own "When Harry Met Sally" moment. You know the moment I'm talking about; the moment they break up with you, tell you "it's not you, it's me," that they're not ready for a committed relationship, but if they were, you would be the one; that moment when they tell you that the timing wasn't right, and that if it were only a year from now, things would be different, or that lame, sad excuse of "I don't want to fall in love right now, and you scare me because I could fall in love with you in an instant." I'm ready to throw up now, because it's happened to me, and I'm sure at one time or another, it's happened to you. The worst part of those times is that we buy all that bullshit. We listen, we understand, and we almost feel badly for "them!" We still make excuses to our friends who tell us to "kick them to the curb," by saying "but they were honest, and really didn't mean to upset me." Oh, boy, if I had a nickel for every stupid line I bought, I'd be one rich woman.

There will come that moment when you realize you got played by them in a big way; that moment when you just want to crawl under a rock and hide from your friends that you humiliated yourself to by making excuses for them. You want to hide from the truth, that at that moment, you were too blind to see. And you know when that time is? It's when "Harry Met Sally" meets "you and your ex!" It's that time when you see or hear that your ex is with someone else; that suddenly they're ready for the commitment they couldn't and wouldn't give you. All the things you wanted that, they wouldn't give you are the things they're willingly giving to someone else. And they're giving freely, willingly, and full force!

Our first thought would be to wish everything bad on them, send karma on her way to get them, and hope that their heart get's bashed to bits. Once we realize that would be bad karma for us, we realize what the problem really is. And it's simple…

You wonder "why wasn't I good enough for them to do all those things for me?"

Go ahead, have your pity party and low self esteem bashing for a few minutes. Done? I am...with my own Harry. Of course you're feeling hurt, not because of a broken heart, but because someone else got what you felt you deserved and what you wanted. Someone else got everything you were willing to wait for in minutes; well, it feels like minutes.

Now, let's get down to the heart of it. You don't know the person they're with now, as in most cases, or may know something of them. It doesn't matter, you knew "them." And you start thinking "what was wrong with me?" Answer: nothing. Next answer: THEM! That's what was wrong, they weren't right for you. Yet still, we stand and look in the mirror and suddenly can pick out every flaw that we never saw before: the hair, the wrinkles the clothes, the everything. Having gone through this myself, my best advice to you is STOP RIGHT THERE! Look in the mirror at your beauty, your light, and see the wonderful heart inside of you. Obviously, they're not seeing that in you; they're seeing another pretty face or hotter body, and that is what feeds their ego. You didn't feed their ego; the new person is, and feeding the ego is a recipe for disaster.

"The worst thing you can do for yourself is feed your ego;
The best thing you can do for yourself is nourish your
self-esteem."

In most cases, women tend to feed a man's ego, while men tend to starve a woman's self esteem. This isn't always the case, but more often than not, it is. This isn't anything new; it's been going on throughout history. Men need to feel like men, and sadly, more and more men are products of their ego, and you will never have all that you deserve from them if that's the type they are.

In a perfect world, we would all love ourselves for who we are, and would be able to look ourselves in the mirror and see the beauty in front of us. The reality is that the world isn't perfect and neither are we. So it becomes, as it should be, our responsibility to love ourselves and nourish our self-esteem. Once you can do this, you will attract a partner who will help nourish it for you, just as you would nourish their self-esteem. Love is a two way street that doesn't work well when you're both going in different directions.

Let them be with someone new and offer all the things to someone else that they didn't give you. It could be, although I doubt it, that they fell in love. The question is: will this new person love them back, and whose heart will get broken now? My guess would be "their heart." Karma get's us all just when she needs to, and someone like that will eventually have her knocking at their door.

Stop feeling badly that you weren't "good enough for them;" the truth is "you were too good for them" all along.

"Ignorance and Bliss"

"It takes but one moment of ignorance to cost you a lifetime of bliss."

So much for that old saying "ignorance is bliss." I haven't met anyone who believes that. If you do, you're denying yourself the truth. I would imagine that there are many people who would argue that there are some things they would rather not know, but I'm not one of them. I feel that "truth" is necessary to make the right decisions for yourself so that you are able to have and live the life you want. Anything less is based on a lie.

This rings true for relationships, your health, or your job, to name a few. Suppose you're hired for a job, and a week or month into it you find out that you now have to work three hours later a week for the same pay. Wouldn't you have wanted to know that sooner? It could have been the difference between that job and another one that may have been better for you.

How about that special person you met and can envision a future with? Would it make a difference that they didn't tell you they weren't divorced yet, or that the decision to divorce happened while they were with you? Wouldn't you have wanted to know? You may have dated them anyway, yet the important thing is that you would have known that they were honest. Now you're questioning their integrity, and yet again, you may have gotten involved in a relationship that prevented you from having a different and better one.

Think about my breast cancer. Trust me, not having a mammogram for five years, then finding a lump was my truest example and lesson on how my ignorance could have cost me a lifetime of bliss… or a lifetime at all. Strangely, the year before I found my tumor I had a sinking feeling that I probably had cancer. I used to think it was just my fear talking to my stupidity about not getting checked; yet the fears rang true, and I will say, I thank God I caught it early, went through the treatments, and was blessed to become a survivor.

Do you understand the point I'm trying to make? Not knowing the truth can hurt, but the lies will always hurt worse.

"The truth is free; lies will cost you a price."

That goes for your own truth and lies as well as someone else's.

We don't always catch someone else in a lie until it's too late, and then we are forced to make the decision of whether the lie was forgivable or not. We ask ourselves if it was really that big of a lie or one that you could let sneak on by. Yet a lie is a lie.

"Everything is forgivable, yet not always repairable."

The truth is that everything IS forgivable, but is it ever the same? Lies will cause damage, big and small, and once a lie is told and found out, things just aren't the same. You may say you appreciate finding out the truth after all, yet wouldn't you have been happier if there was no lie to begin with? You see, this is where our value of ourselves becomes more important than not. If you truly value yourself, do you want someone who didn't value or respect you enough to be honest in your life?

Let's face it, we lie, they lie, and we may be living with someone who has lied to us before. Yet ask yourself this: was the damage caused by the lie repairable, or simply forgivable? Did it change your trust for them?

I was in a situation once in which I was the one being lied to; untruths were being told about me so that the people involved wouldn't know the truth about this person. It was a ripple effect of lies. Once I knew about the lies, I confronted the person and after a lengthy discussion, chose to believe them. There, I thought to myself, I finally got the truth after the lies had been found out; that settled that, because they came clean. That feeling lasted all of five seconds before my mind started thinking "was he just lying about the lie to get out of it?" You see, trust was broken, deception abound, and even if they were finally telling the truth, I would always question that. Needless to say, my choice was to let them go and move on.

The same goes with your own self. Are you honest with yourself? Do you know your truth? As I said earlier, I was living in a state of ignorance for five years, knowing that while I should have had a mammogram, I chose not to. I often look back and wonder why I didn't just go and get one, yet through talking with other women, it seems that many of us felt the same way. It's the fear of the unknown that prevents us from going; we don't want to know what we may need to know. It's an ignorance of a different kind, but a lie to our self. I am grateful that my tumor was found and treated, and I try every day now never to live in a state of ignorance. My ignorance could have cost me my life, and that price would have been based on my denying my own truth. I still have moments of ignoring things that need attention, but something or someone always pops up in my life to remind me to face whatever it is. There are no accidents or coincidences, simply "messages" that a Higher Power is trying to get through to us.

Ignorance is not bliss and bliss is not found through ignorance. Truth, from those around you, and more importantly, from yourself, is the only way to make the choices that need to be made for your highest good.

"If you should find yourself getting hit hard with the truth, at least let it knock some sense into you."

"Pulling the Trigger"

Throughout my journey of getting to know myself better, I have found that there is one area that needs much more work: triggers. They put me right into "defense mode" for myself, and although I know better than that, it still can be a difficult task to get through.

What is a trigger? It's that one small thing (and in some cases, more than one) that someone says or does to you that brings up painful memories, and has the potential to bring out the absolute worst in you; at least for me that's how it works.

I went through a difficult situation on the day of my breast cancer surgery; it was my friend who was soon to be the gun that held all the triggers. Sadly our definition of "friendship" was completely different.

My definition of a friend is fairly universal: you're both there for each other when they need you and even when they don't. You love them, respect them, laugh and cry with them, and are loyal to one another. My friend's definition of what a friend is supposed to be was simply whoever was available to be around when no one else was; there was no love, respect, laughter, or loyalty when someone else entered the picture. See the difference? I would soon learn this the hard way, and the day of my surgery was not really the time to learn.

The short version is this: they forgot about my surgery and their commitment to my children and me to help us out through my recovery. Why did they forget, you ask? A friend never turns their back on you when you ask for their help, right? Well, I guess they never learned this. So, moving forward, why did they forget? It was because someone walked into their life and took the place of my role in the friendship. That relationship lasted two months, until they came running back to me when it ended. They ran back to their only friend…or so they thought.

Herein lies' the triggers; as we spent weeks discussing their crappy behavior, and that I don't need friends like that in my life, they will still bring up things about my past and throw them at me like darts. People that do that to you are, in my opinion, the ones' that refuse to take accountability for their actions, and it's to throw blame elsewhere. I'd say that they lost the right to do that; the past is the past. Yet, they'd point that gun, bring up something, and bamm! The trigger of that difficult time ripped through like a bullet.

Enough with my venting; follow me here.

I learned many things throughout my journey with cancer, and the biggest lesson I learned is that I didn't love myself as much as I should have. I let people say and do what they wanted to me, and while it may have made me angry or hurt, I rarely spoke up about it. I believe that all of those things I didn't say were packed away in the tumor in my breast. That tumor held all my feelings of hurt, anger, low self-esteem and sadness.

Cancer taught me to change all of that. No, I didn't turn into a bitch over night, or even now, yet what I did do was find my voice; "***my*** voice."

Aside from giving birth to five children, fighting cancer was the biggest thing I had to do in my life so far, and I decided that it would be "my way or the highway." There were a few close friends and several family members that I had to say good bye to, at least until I got through this battle. They were much too negative and I was much too positive. And it worked; a year after the tumor was found and I began using my voice, I was also cancer free!

Yet, today, there are still moments I'll battle the "triggers," and I realized that there's no need to. It's simple: my ex-friend was never truly my friend; I was a matter of convenience, and taken for granted, so after all I've learned, why were there still triggers from them? Answer: I allowed it.

You see, I believe that what we allow is what will continue, and throughout the last few months of this behavior, the light finally came on. Why am I allowing them the right to speak to me, let alone be in my life, when they certainly proved that they didn't belong there, or even earn the right to?

I'm not. I stopped allowing it. And so begins the closure and ending of a friendship; then again, maybe it's more of the awakening to realize that they never were my friend at all. Yet why would I hurt for someone like that? It's not hurting over losing them; it's hurting over being good to someone who gave you that "slap in the face" of the reality of knowing that not everyone is nice, not everyone is a good friend, and not everyone will treat us the way we treat them. It's a cold hard fact to face, yet another lesson to learn along the journey.

You're the only one who can get rid of the proverbial gun; and if you don't, you open the door to allow someone else to pull the trigger.

"It's Time to Say Good-Bye"

Letting go isn't easy and clinging to the memories of something or someone that is no longer in your life is even harder. It's never good to allow yourself to stay stuck in a situation for too long. The more time you allow to pass by not letting go of something only brings more pain, anger, and questions which you'll never have an answer to.

When life changes, and relationships of all types end, we're left feeling hurt. The hurt turns into anger, the anger into disappointment that things didn't go as you had planned, or worse, had hoped. Yet the longer you give your mind the power and control to feel those negative emotions, the more you're missing out on some wonderful things.

Change isn't always easy, yet it's always worth it. Think for a moment about the situation you may be stuck in. You are the one feeling those negative emotions, while the other person most likely isn't. They moved on to a new chapter of their life while you didn't, and for each day that passes in which you continue to think and feel upset about it, is another day you've given your control to them.

Everyone has to grieve the loss of a friend, relationship or job, yet allowing that grief to go on for too long becomes a completely different situation; you've now allowed yourself to become stuck in a vortex of bad feelings.

So what do you do to get out of that vortex?

I believe we all do the same thing, until we realize that one thing isn't the answer: we move backwards, searching for those feelings of excitement and happiness we had in our past. We may reconnect with old friends who have long been out of the picture, tried doing things we used to that brought us excitement in our past, and doing anything and everything we can to forget about the task at hand: letting go, moving on, and saying good-bye.

I've done it myself at times, yet throughout my own spiritual journey I've learned the signs of moving backwards; I've been taught the process of letting go; I've learned, albeit difficult, how to forgive the other person and how to forgive myself. Yet now I watch so many around me doing what I had done long ago, and while I know I can share my experiences of moving on with them, I can't tell them how they need to do it. They must learn on their own.

So how do you watch someone you love spend every day still holding onto the hurt someone has caused them? How do you stand by and do nothing?

Well, you're not doing nothing by doing nothing. You can listen, you can stand by them, you can offer support, but you also have a choice to make as well: how long are you going to do this for? When will **you** have had enough?

I watch those around me trying to numb their pain in any way they can. They self-medicate, they try to find feelings from their past that are no longer there; they try to re-create the "old days" without an ounce of realization of what's in front of them: "life."

They lose sight of all the wonderful people, places and things they have in this part of their life simply because they can't say good-bye to the less than wonderful people, places and things from their past. The tragedy of this is that inevitably, as they stay stuck much too long, they will lose what they had all along in their present life: the good things that are right in front of their face. They will lose love from those who loved them through this ugly situation that has lasted too long. The longer it takes for them to say good bye to the past puts all that they have now at risk. They don't realize that the person who's there with them now is beginning to hurt, and will eventually begin their own process of moving on.

So you see, you can take all the time you want to let go of a situation that hurt you, but keep in mind, while paying attention to that, you're not paying attention to someone that really cares.

While you're busy going "outside" of the relationship or situation you're living in to find that "old" feeling to help you through, you're telling that person who's there for you now, and quite loudly, that only your past lives can help; your present life can't… and that's a cold hard fact that you may have to face. Don't lose someone you love because of someone who no longer loves you.

It's time to say good-bye to the old and hello to the good things life has handed you. Remember this: "life is what happens when you're not paying attention." Pay attention before it's too late, because by the time you're done getting over the past your present may already be out the door.

I beg of you to let go of the people, places, situations and struggles that no longer serve you. Let **them** go before the life you are in, one filled with love and laughter and living, lets **you** go.

"Letting Go"

I've come to realize that in order to live the best possible life, we have to step back and take an inventory of our lives. This entails really looking at how we're living our life and who we allow in it. It's that "inventory" that forces us to think about why life may not be as happy and joyful, healthy or as peaceful as we want it to be. We can achieve all those great things, yet it takes work, and sometimes it takes letting some things go…and that includes people as well.

Letting go is just about the hardest thing we ever have to do, but speaking from experience, is so worth the time and effort.

Drinking, smoking, excessive eating, toxic friends, family or relationships, bad behaviors… the list can go on forever, yet these are all things that do not serve our highest good; not for our health or our emotional well being.

So how do we let go? Do we just say it then do it? Do we falsely trick ourselves into believing that we've already done it? You see, letting go involves several steps, and I'll tell you now, it's not easy as you may think.

Addictions are difficult to overcome, and I'm not just talking about chemical addictions. Everything, physical or emotional, that isn't for our highest good is an addiction, a pattern we've allowed ourselves to live in and around. Addictions are simply us giving control to the demon, and that includes our thought process and behaviors as well.

Life is a habit, a routine, and just as easily as we find ourselves living in them, it's not as easy to release them. Once we truly make the choice to take back our control and change our life to one that serves our highest good, we must decide what we need to "let go" of.

We live in these "addictions" because they become comfortable, and it's what we know. It's "living inside the box, not out of it." We have to be conscious of our comfort zones, because while they may feel comfortable, they're not always comforting.

"Sometimes we have to do something uncomfortable to actually become comfortable."

I believe with all my heart that some things that come to us too easily aren't worth having, and they don't last for long. It's a short lived whirlwind of happiness and comfort, soon to leave because we hadn't done the work, or given it the correct thought process as to WHY we needed the change.

We're all given the intuition, or "gut feeling" that tells us what we should or shouldn't be doing. We know we shouldn't be smoking, or drinking too much; we preach to our children that they shouldn't do drugs; we tell our friends that the toxic relationship they're in is bad for them, yet, as creatures of comfort and habit, we don't take the time to recognize this in ourselves.

And why is this? Because we're creatures of habit, and we spend more time thinking about the things that those we love need to let go of, instead of what WE have to let go of. And you know what the irony is? We need to let go of loving others more than we love ourselves. When we can do that, suddenly we'll be able to see what WE need to let go of, and those very people we voice our opinions to about what THEY need to let go of may actually be one of the things we need to let go of to move forward.

"Letting go is the only way of moving forward."

So let's talk about how to go about letting go, or at least how to begin to. There is no "right or wrong" way to let go, and there is no time frame of how quickly or long it may take; the time is up to you, as well as what you consider the right way to do it. The one piece of advice I can give you based on my personal moments of "letting go" is this: the moment you love yourself completely and unconditionally is the defining moment of seeing and knowing yourself for who you are. Once you can do that, you'll know to your toes what and who you need to let go of. I say this with all the love in my heart to you, and while I know the journey of letting go is often difficult, trust me when I say this: it is so worth it!

The first step is to identify what we need to let go of. Bad habits such as smoking and drinking are easy to identify because we know that they're bad for our health. Healthy choices are easy to make, yet often harder to do, especially when it's due to an addiction. The good news is that there are doctors, centers, patches and gum to help ward off these ugly habits. These are the "no brainers" that we see warning commercials and advertisements about, yet until we make the decision to release them, it'll never happen.

There's one thing I've learned about addictions, and the lesson came from Dr. Wayne Dyer. He wrote a short story on loving your addictions as you release them, because in the end, they taught you a lot about yourself; and he's right, no matter the addiction.

The next step would be to find a spot where you are able to silence your mind; a place that calms you and fills you with peace. These are the places that clear your mind and free your soul to think long and hard about your life. These are the moments of clarity as to why your life isn't quite the way you want it. Don't put pressure on yourself, because it may take a few times to find that clarity, or it may come to you right away.

But trust me, the clarity and the answers will come; they always do and at just the right moment and time they need to.

As far as the "people" in our life, well, that can be tough, especially if it's a romantic partner, a child, a parent or family member or your best friend. There's no easy way to put this, so I'm just going to give it to you straight: if anyone, for any reason, brings you pain, is abusive, controlling, or condescending, if anyone in your life makes you feel "less" of who you are and makes you question yourself, if they don't bring out the best in you then it's time to LET THEM GO! That doesn't mean you don't love them, it just means you love yourself more, and that's how it should be. It doesn't mean that you never have to speak to them again, but less is more. It means that they can't be in your life on a daily basis, and for some, on any basis, and while it's tough to cut the cords with some people, it's necessary for you to be healthy and happy. One of my favorite phrases from "Eat, Pray, Love" by Elizabeth Gilbert is "so miss 'em, wish 'em love and light, then drop it." I've lived by that mantra ever since the first time I saw the movie and read the book.

I've let family members and friends go, and while it was difficult, it wasn't a process that was hurtful or hateful, it simply "was." My life seemed to change overnight when I let go of the toxicity, the stress, and the drama they caused. You need to believe that it's okay to put yourself first. The way you feel about yourself and your life affects all those around you. When you love yourself as you love others, all that good stuff will spill onto those around you! It's quite the "domino" effect!

Once you've identified what you need to let go of, take a deep breath and do it. Make it a small ritual, do something special just for the occasion, but do something! This is the mental part of letting go, and this is the hardest. For me, I sit out in the sun or under the stars, and close my eyes. I take several deep breaths, and in my mind I tell myself "I let go of this person who brings negative energy to my life; I wish them love and joy as I let them go, and while I may miss them,

I know that this is how it's meant to be." You can find what's comfortable for you, and say more or say less. After all, this is YOUR "letting go ritual," not theirs. Are you wondering how you'll know if it works? For me, I know it's worked after I've sat in silence and repeated the words in my mind, and tears start flowing. My body feels as though a weight has been lifted. I believe the tears are my soul's way of releasing the person or situation which was not the best for me; that the tears are that sweet, gentle release of being able to surrender something that wasn't good for me. The tears are my soul's way of telling me that I just learned to love myself!

Let the tears flow for the loss, let the tears flow for the joy, and let the tears prove that you have just felt an amazing wealth of love for yourself, the same type as you have always felt for others.

Letting go is the only way of moving forward; holding onto a painful past prevents us from living in a loving present; letting go doesn't mean we need to forget, it means that we simply need to forgive it and move on.

Yes, doors will close, and that may bring fear. Letting go entails closing a door, or several, yet I believe a leap of faith and getting rid of the fear will get you through, because:

"When one door closes, put on your boots and kick the French doors open!"

"Moving Forward"

"You can't move forward if you're standing still."

I know of many people, myself included, that get so frustrated with life at times that all they seem to say is "I just can't seem to move forward in my life. I feel like I'm stuck."

And they are…stuck, that is.

I've been there, you've been there, we've all been there, yet I've learned through many teachers and situations that just because we "feel" stuck, doesn't always mean that we "are" stuck. It only means that we are standing still, plain and simple.

No one is stuck; not me, not you, not anyone. We just feel that way at times, simply because we're standing still in the middle of what should be the past, not knowing how to move forward from it. There's no science to it, yet it can be a difficult process, especially when you don't realize what you need to move on from. On the other hand, you may be painfully aware of why you're stuck. The problem for you is that you don't know how to move from the past, the person, or the situation.

It's not always easy moving forward, especially when we're leaving someone or something behind that is "comfortable." Life is ever changing, and the older we get, the more things change. No one ever said change was easy…or did they? Personally, I love change! I love the excitement of not knowing what's coming next, or where life is about to take me. It's a nervous kind of excitement, yet what I know for sure is I couldn't feel this way if I didn't have faith. Without faith, there'd be nothing but fear, and no matter what life hands me, I refuse to allow fear into my thoughts or behaviors.

"With faith there is hope; with fear there is nothing."

I'm not saying that fear doesn't come into my thoughts once in a great while, but I will not and choose not to allow it to stay for long. I believe in the Law of Attraction in that what you think and believe is what you attract, and fear is no exception. Fear, in a mild dose, reminds us of how strong we really are because we are able to understand the fear and release it. We're able to let it go. Trust me, you wouldn't be normal if you weren't afraid every so often. The problem you'll have is if you stay in a constant state of fear. That's something that will most assuredly hold you in your past and make you feel stuck.

ANNE DENNISH

Relationships, jobs, illnesses, you name it, fear can find it. Fear is normal, but nothing good comes from it. It brings anxiety, depression, illness and stress, to name a few, and fear is what plants our feet into the ground as if we're dropped in cement and can't move. Fear will keep you stuck; fear will prevent you from moving forward; fear will keep at you until you get rid of it. You may not think you're strong enough to deal with ridding yourself of fear, yet you are.

"When you think you can't find the strength, the strength will find you."

Sometimes all you have to do is let go of the fear, and you'll find yourself stronger than you had imagined. I believe strength is in us all, and sometimes it takes a smack of fear, or a life changing moment to wake us up and realize our strength was there all along. If you can't find your strength, take a breath and let it find you. Trust me on this, it's there, and I speak from experience.

"Going through tough times doesn't make you stronger; it makes you realize just how strong you were all along."

You have to let go of the past in order to move forward, and that's a fact. You can't stay locked into the past and expect to move throughout the journey of your life. Try viewing life as an adventure, with good and bad throughout it. Everything that happens to you has something to teach you about yourself. Make your life an exciting journey, even amidst the mundane tasks of the day. You don't need a million dollars to do it, you don't need to travel all over the world; you need a mind and spirit that takes a stand for your life, makes it your own, views it as an exciting journey filled with adventure, and does what it takes to keep fear at bay.

"Let go of the past; walk in your present; and glide into your future."

If you can do these things, you'll be amazed at all that life has to offer. Miracles happen, dreams are fulfilled, and life is truly lived when you change your perspective. No one can change it for you; it's all up to you! It's your choice; better yet, it's your chance… a chance for anything and everything you want! Take those fears and face them head on with strength, determination and faith that all things along the road of your life's journey are happening just as they should.

"Make your life an adventure…"

"The Truth Seeker"

I'm a truth seeker; I will spend more time on finding out the truth than most people. I despise lies and deception, and if you're ignorant enough to think I believe you, then you'll soon learn to be very smart because I won't let you get away with it.

I'm sure no one likes to be lied to, and while there may be an occasion or two where you're better off not knowing the truth, then you better make sure you cover it, bury it, and lie good enough to make sure I never find out. I'd say that comes under the category of "lying by omission;" I'd say it's more of "lying so that you don't get your ass kicked when I find out."

Are there times to lie? Maybe there are, yet then again, maybe not.

A lie can change the course of your life. When someone lies to you, they take away your right to the make the best decisions for yourself, and vice versa. The truth can hurt, and it can break a heart into a million pieces. Yet, should that happen, at least you're able to think about it and put the lie into perspective, along with the person that lied to you. Once the initial shock and hurt wear off a bit, your common sense and dignity return, and that is where you find yourself able to look at the situation and make the right decisions for yourself. It's at that point that it's no longer about the liar, but about the one lied to: YOU!

That is why I'm a truth seeker. I've fought many battles throughout my life so far, and in the truth of "loving myself" more, I need to know the truth. A lie can all too easily allow me to make the wrong decisions for my highest good, while the truth will allow the right ones to be made.

Here's an example of how I wasted several months of my time and effort because of a lie, yet then again, nothing really is a waste of time, because there are times it may take us months to see the whole picture. That's what I realized throughout this extremely painful process.

Here comes the lesson I would soon learn the extremely hard way…I let an ex-friend back in my life for two months of conversations. Most would call me crazy, but I'm a believer that all things happen for a reason, and while I may have used the term "wasted my time and effort for two months" it wasn't a waste at all. I learned more about them and much more about me, and I realized this: I don't need people like that in my life, and in fact, they were the ultimate chameleon and liar.

What they did was despicable.

Was I stupid? Not really. I was about to start three weeks of radiation, so I took the easy way out, I let them hang around me to explain their behavior. Yet throughout those weeks, those months, I realized that while "everything is forgivable, it's not always repairable." They broke a trust, a friendship, a family, and almost broke me by their behavior.

If one of my friends told me this happened to them, the first thing I would tell them is to "run, don't walk!" Sometimes we give others the best advice, yet never take it ourselves. It took me two months to finally come to terms with all of this. I don't deserve a friend like that, and more importantly I don't want a friend like that.

Saying we "deserve" something almost sounds too easy; saying "we want" something shows a type of strength we've found in ourselves by putting ourself first, and owning who we are and what we will allow.

I made the decision to end the friendship, and it wasn't easy. We have been friends for a long time, yet the behavior and lack of respect towards me showed me who they really are; and that is no one I ever thought them to be.

The lesson is easy: sometimes it takes time along with a clear heart and mind to see what's right in front of us. We always know the answer deep down inside of us, yet sometimes we have to wait until the heart catches up to what the mind already knows.

Don't beat yourself up for learning the hard way; good things come through hard work, and nothing worth having comes easy.

"Thinking"

Funny how you can be in a situation and suddenly someone says something to you that get's you thinking. That happens to me all the time, and when it does, a story is typically born. So I was surprised that it happened again…and I love those moments to think outside the box, to let my mind ponder on the question, to have to find my own answer to someone's question. This story was born out of this question:

"You've told me your strengths, now what are your weaknesses?"

I sat and looked him right in the face. Are you kidding me? My weaknesses? I've spent the last few years building up the self-esteem that two bad marriages hurt, learning to accept that it's alright to love myself, realizing and believing that I have every right to be happy, and that I deserve to be treated with kindness and respect. I learned that I'm not selfish to say "I'm worth more than that, and I'm well deserving of it." I used to believe those statements were nothing more than vanity talking, but I've learned it's not. It's loving yourself as much as you love the people in your life.

So why was this person asking me to drum up my weaknesses? I thought I had made my weaknesses my strength…

"My strength is their weakness, my weakness their strength."

This question stuck in my head the entire drive home. What was my weakness? Okay, let's see…I'm easy going, and at times too easy going. People easily take advantage of me for that. Check…there's one. Moving on, let's find another one. Alright, I tend to give more of myself to others than I do myself. Everyone always comes first, and I get what's left. Check, check…there's two. Now, what's one more? I thought and I thought. Suddenly, it was if I was hit by a lightning bolt and the light came on. I love with abandon, with passion, and with everything that I am. Check, check, check! Weakness? Absolutely, because I love everyone in my life that I'm blessed to have in it, and there are times I've learned over the years that you can love too much. My feeling is this: if I'm blessed enough to have you in my life, I can promise you that you will feel blessed by my love for you and my willingness to be there for you.

Quite an eye opener, that question. Yet as I thought about it all night, and as I'm writing about it now, I've realized that these "weaknesses", as some may call it, are in fact, my "strengths." They are the pieces of me that make me who I am, and I would assume are the reason I have so many wonderful people in my life. I believe that "some people come in your life as blessings, some come in as lessons." No matter what brings someone into my life, I believe that they were meant to be in it, for whatever amount of time they're supposed to be. I don't waste time on wondering why they're here, but embrace the time that they are.

So, as for my weaknesses? Yes, I have a few, maybe even more, but you know what? I don't look at them as a sign of my weakness; I see them as a sign of my strength.

"The Ultimate Test of Trust"

After a 20 year marriage that blessed me with five children, and a second marriage that lasted less than five years, I find myself in unchartered territory: I'm living with the man I love. I've never lived with anyone before, and never thought I believed in it. Yet as my mind will ponder all aspects of my life, this one is no exception. So I began thinking about my "living arrangements" and this man that I believe is the love of my life. Why do I have a moment of worry that he might leave? Why, after two marriages ended, does the "m" word pop up? It's not that I want to be married again, although my thinking may change over time. Yet, what is it that stirs up this high school feeling of "I hope we'll never break up?" I realized what it was: it's that way of thinking that was embedded into my head since I was a child: you grow up, you get married, and you'll live happily ever after.

That is so not true. Two marriages didn't last, and there certainly was no happily ever after involved when the divorces were final, yet I realized something: falling in love for the last time in my life, living together with no ring or wedding, was a test of who I've become and how much I've grown in my life. This was the ultimate "test of trust."

There, I said it out loud, and once you put it out there, you're one step closer to working on the issue at hand: trust.

Some days I think it would be easier to be married, that once you took those vows no one can leave you, yet I've proved it to myself twice that "yes, they can leave, and so can you."

So I sit here, day after day, wondering why I have a moment of feeling insecure. Is it because the relationship is wonderful, happy, and that we both are truly soul mates and best friends? Why should I be worried, when it's all so right?

The answer is simple: because I've gone through hell and back many times to get to this lovely, earthly feeling of heaven with this man; because it's a blessing I thought could never be found, and because he allowed me to know what love truly is. He's allowed me the freedom and the safety of being just who I am, and loves me for it.

And then I had my "waking up" moment. I realized that as much as I preach to people that every situation we go through and every person that crosses our paths brings a lesson to learn about ourselves that makes us stronger, this was my lesson. My moment was to learn to trust 100%, and no less. All the things I say to others and write about revolves around love of oneself and complete trust in our intuition, and that when fear creeps in, all bets are off. There's no place for fear, simply faith, and faith is just another form of "trust" in yourself and those you surround yourself with.

"The ultimate test of trust is love."

The task of trust is at hand, and I know to my toes that I've no reason to fear the place I'm in. The love he and I share is stronger than any negative or dark forces around us that try and sabotage it. I know that if something bad can penetrate what we share, then it wasn't what I thought it was in the first place.

Cancer didn't scare me nearly as much as falling in love for the first and last time in my life. It didn't happen easily for either of us, as we both began this relationship as deeply wounded beings. Our hearts had been broken to the point that neither of us thought we'd love again, that perhaps all these wonderful things we hear about love are simply written in books. Yet despite a rocky start, we stuck with it, and throughout the first few months the cement walls which we both had surrounding our hearts for years began to crumble. It wasn't easy, and it didn't happen quickly, yet it happened, piece by piece. We learned to trust one another, because we knew if we didn't, we'd be nothing.

Now I find myself living with this amazing man and my children, building a life amongst both our families, and feeling overwhelmed at how many wonderful things have happened in and around our lives because of this love we have for one another.

My "ultimate test of trust" is one I'm passing, and so is he. I think it's healthy to have a brief moment of insecurity, if for no reason than for us to stop and think what it is that's bothering us and why we feel that way. Most times it's nothing in the relationship, but simply a piece of us that's out of balance, allowing a negative force to take hold. No good comes from the dark. Allowing it in for too long will bring exactly what it came to steal, and we must be smart enough to erase it from our mind and surround ourselves with the light of love and trust, faith and hope, happiness and joy.

I choose to believe these moments are the Universe testing and reminding us of how far we've come along our journey of life, and reminding us never to lose sight of the light; to guard and shield ourselves against the dark.

I've learned many lessons while living my "life journey" and I know in my heart that we should never stop learning; it's the lessons that make us a better person and allow us to find a strength we may never have known.

"There is no dancing in the dark, only in the light."

Yes, just when I thought it was near perfect, I felt a twinge of the darkness. I allowed it in for just a little while, because in the end, we have a choice to sit in the darkness, or dance in the light. I chose to select my thoughts carefully, ask my Higher Power to place a wall of protection around us, and figure out why it was allowed in the first place.

It was the "ultimate test of trust" and I have decided to pass this with flying colors. After all, there's no love to be found in the dark, only in the light, and I would much rather be dancing through this beautiful life in the light!

"Time Frame"

I can't begin to tell you how many times people have told me to "take it slow, don't rush things, just wait." My usual answer to their unsolicited advice is this: "why?"

Are relationships and dreams measured in a time frame? Are you supposed to wait for a determined period of time before the dream comes true or the relationship goes to the next level?

Is life in general measured in a "time frame?"

I say "no," absolutely not. Life is meant to be lived, day by day, moment by moment. Time is fleeting, and as we grow older, we begin to realize just how quickly time begins to pass. It certainly flies by quicker than when we were younger. We couldn't wait for time to pass when we were younger! As we get older, we'd like it to slow down. Yet that should be our only "time frame;" that we want more of it, and not for us to move more slowly throughout our lives. We want more hours, more days, and more years, yet as we grow, we realize that time is precious. It's to be honored, loved and respected, because you never know when you'll run out of it.

So why go slow? Why wait?

The people that say this to me are the ones who live unhappy lives; they're not content with they're own. They live in a fear of someone else having what they never could find, so they tell me to slow down and take it easy.

My life has been a journey of ups and downs, ins and outs, topping it off with surviving breast cancer, so I'm not slowing down, I'm not taking it easy, I'm going for the brass ring, because that's what life is: LIVING!

Life hands you many surprises, from a job that you never expected, or a relationship that fell into your life. And what's our first instinct? It's usually to play it safe and be careful. We tell ourselves not to get too excited, because what happens if something goes wrong?"

So what if something *does* go wrong?

WAKING UP

What's the worst that can happen? You get hurt? You lose the job? So what! It was meant to happen, it was meant to teach you something. Pay attention, because I believe with all my heart that everything happens for a reason, and there's a reason for everything that happens: it's to teach us more about ourselves so that we can keep moving forward into a life that we want.

So why slow down? "Fear" slows us down, "fear" makes us cautious and nervous, and truth be told, "fear" stops us from receiving some amazing things that come knocking at our door!

Don't let fear "inter-fear" with your life!

Fear makes us want to go slow, and quite frankly, fear is the easy way out to not try something new, give something a chance, or simply go into unchartered territory!

Faith, my friends, is the way to go, the way to live. Fear has no place when you are trying something new; faith lives in that place.

I'm not saying fear doesn't step in where it's needed, yet I choose to believe it's not so much "fear" but our intuition, our little voice inside, that cautions us to do or not do something. It's not fear, it's a gut response.

"Fear" prevents you from moving forward; "intuition" let's you know if it's safe.

I lived a long time fearful of the unknown, of taking chances, of stepping out of the box, but with each new lesson learned, with each broken heart or disappointment, I began to learn to step out of the box a bit more, to take those chances, and to risk what might come of it. It didn't happen overnight, and took years of practice, a handful of great spiritual teachers, and many different people and situations dropping in and out of my life to teach me that. I know now that life "outside the box" is so much more fulfilling than life "inside it."

I can't promise you that you'll never get hurt or be disappointed, that what you believed to be true at the time turned out not to be true at all, but I can promise you that you will learn from it if you choose, and that you can take that experience and heal into an even stronger person.

"Trials, tribulations and blessings are the secret to life because you can't have one without the other."

I'm a believer that "you've gotta go through hell to get to heaven" and until we leave this Earth, that's what we have to do. The world can be a crazy place, and God knows there's a lot to be afraid of, yet if you live in a constant state of fear, in that time warp of "taking it slow," then you'll never attract what you want, just what you believe: fear.

For those of you who have children, don't you teach them to go for their dreams? Shoot for the moon? That they'll never know unless they try? Sure you do, yet as parents we forget that applies to us as well.

So go for it, slow down only if you're tired and need to rest, and let life happen! Fall in love, take a chance, risk getting hurt, do it all, and never look back. Look forward!

"You can't move forward if you're still looking back."

Yes, the past is a part of us all. It's because of our past that we are who we are in the present, and even our future self will look different down the line. We grow every day, believe it or not, and what we look like in the now may look much better in the future. Isn't that what we're here for? To be the best we can for those we love, and most importantly, for our self.

What's happening in your life at this moment? Did you just start a new job or leave one? Did one of your children move out or is your marriage ending? Are you falling in love?

The list can go on, but change is inevitable, and while we may feel fearful, feel that for a brief moment, and then let it go. The moment you feel fear is the moment you know to let it go and find your faith, and if you can do that, then you will know you have learned a thing or two in your life so far. Fear can ring the bell, but you don't have to answer it; proceed with caution as you see it outside your door, then walk away.

"Let fear check you in to faith."

Everything in life happens as it should, when it should, and the only control we have over things is our perception of it, how we handle it, and what we allow it to make us feel. You're stronger than you think, and that I know for sure. We're all stronger than we believe ourselves to be; we become "human" at times and forget that. Yet at what we may believe is our weakest moment, our falling from grace, our hitting bottom, someone or something may suddenly drop in your life; it's what they call Divine Timing. You just gotta believe!

"When you can't find the strength, let the strength find you."

The strength will always find you; it has no time frame, and while you may be sitting around waiting for it to come, I promise you it will. And it may come in ways you had never imagined, and that's a beautiful thing.

So today, let fear check you into faith, and go! Take the risk, take the chance, make a change and go for it! Forget the "time frame!" Life is for the living, and if you take things too slowly or cautiously, you just might miss something truly amazing!

Put your running shoes on, hang up the phone on the "time framers" and get moving! You have nothing to lose, and so very much to gain; it's how you look at it!

"Beautiful Boy"

As mothers, we evolve with the changing times as our children grow older, yet once in awhile we change for a reason. My reason to change happened on the night of my son's high school graduation.

Let me start at the beginning. Noah was born three weeks early, weighing in at almost 10 pounds. His labor was short and painful, yet he slid into life and into my arms with all the love and all the answers any mother could hope for.

They placed him in my arms, and of all my five children, he's the only one that looked right into my eyes after making his mark entering this world. His gaze fixed upon mine and it was if that first look between us said, "no worries, Mom, I know more than you think! I got this covered."

Time would prove that to be true again and again. He was born an old soul, and one of the kindest, sweetest, most intuitive people I know. I don't know where my life would have gone if he had not been part of it. He brought out the sweetest part of me, the most ferocious mother bear, and a mother who learned to love with a vengeance.

It was on that graduation night that my sweet boy took me into his 6'3 arms during the many pictures being taken and said "you're part of my picture, Mom. I wouldn't be here without you," and I knew in my heart that he meant it. It was at that moment my heart took a picture to last a lifetime, and I felt emotions that surpassed what I had ever felt before. I realized that the memories of this night would last longer than this lifetime.

After graduation I trekked home, and he followed a few hours later with a bouquet of flowers in his hand for me. Shortly after that he told me, calmly and succinctly as only he could: "Mom, I'm bisexual. I just wanted you to know that."

Well, I would like to say I was shocked and upset, yet I wasn't. I felt peaceful, knowing that he had come to terms with these feelings he had had all throughout his life. He explained to me that his being bisexual wasn't a choice; it's who he is. His choice was when to tell me and the rest of the world. I realized that while most people consider this a "lifestyle," I thought: "don't we all live a certain lifestyle?" I'm divorced and single, raising my children on my own. Doesn't that make me a "lifestyle?" Why would his decision be any different? We all make choices in this life we're living, and it can all change in an instant. So, what did I think and feel? I'll tell you...

I felt proud, relieved, happy, and filled with more love than I thought my heart could hold. My child, my beautiful boy who is so amazing to me, came into his own: turning 18, graduating high school, and making a choice not to hide who he is. I felt nothing but wonderment and love towards him. I knew I was always proud of the amazing boy he was, yet at this moment I found myself more proud of the man he had just become in my eyes.

Yet the news had changed me, and it took a few days before I could figure out how it did. It changed me as a mom; it made me a better mom. More importantly, it made me a better person. Suddenly, I saw things a bit differently; I saw life differently.

It suddenly made me realize how many of us carry labels that say "what" we are, rather than the world seeing "who" we are. I always felt as though people looked at "what" I was before they saw "who" I was. Isn't that how we are when we meet people? We don't ask if a new friend or acquaintance is loyal, kind, or compassionate; we ask if they're married, single, dating, have children, or if and where they work. Do you understand what I mean?

I realized that when I met people I would tell them that I'm a "divorced mother of five and a writer." I always felt that if they wanted to know me more after that "tagline" then they'd try and get to know me. And if they didn't like the "tagline," I wouldn't hear from them again.

I had labeled myself, and vowed from this moment on never to label myself again, and I would never, ever let anyone label my son. He's not a label, he's an amazing man, and that should be what they see: his heart, not his label that society gave him, gave me, and gave all of us. They should see his kindness and his compassion. If the world needs to label people, it should be done by knowing their heart.

His "coming out" allowed me to "come out" as well; out of the darkness, so to speak. I did become a better mother, because during one of our conversations about his decision he told me this: "You gave me the freedom to be who I am, Mom. I couldn't have been this honest with myself if you weren't there for me. You've never judged me and always let me be who I am. So, as much as I struggled with these emotions, you made it easy to accept them and be proud of myself and the life I chose to tell you about."

I couldn't argue that; I had always taught my children to be themselves, and no matter what decisions they made in life, I'd support and love them no matter what.

One of the smartest things my son taught me about this life of his came during a conversation in which I asked him how he knew he was bisexual. I wondered if he had been with a girl and a guy to know his feelings. His response, which to this day blows my mind, was: "When you were growing up, did you have to kiss a guy to know you were heterosexual?"

My first and only answer was: "No." His response: "Then why should I?"

This was another "waking up" moment for me, because he was right, and that was probably the most intelligent way to explain this to me.

It made me a better person because I was able to understand that we all have to make choices, and as my son explained, this has been who he is for his entire life. He simply wasn't ready to make the choice to share this with me, his family, or the world.

I'll tell you the most important thing I learned: my beautiful boy just made the world a better place.

"Fallen Angel"

I believe that everyone one of us has "fallen from grace" at one point or another in our lives. It's that moment when life becomes more than we can handle and we simply find ourselves "lost," unrecognizable to those around us and more importantly, to ourselves. It's that moment of turmoil and pain that determines which direction we take. We fall and stay down, or we fall and work our way back up.

It happens to us all, and it's no reflection of "who" we are. It happens to people with the biggest hearts and kindest of souls; the ones who no one would suspect it could happen to. We fall from grace, and the wonderful person we are suddenly becomes a "fallen angel."

Some believe that those who fall deserve to; that they fell because of the poor choices they made. Those same people believe that once fallen, there is no way that they'll ever get back up; they believe there is no hope. It's a cold hearted way of thinking, yet once again, these are the naysayers, the glass half empty people that can't see past their own selves. They are the ones that have fallen as well, yet they chose not to get up. They don't understand how the kindest of souls can fall, but I do.

They fall because of a heart that takes on the pain of those around them; they are the silent ones that do whatever they can to help someone, yet no one notices that they are hurting as well as the ones they are helping.

At one point or another they were seen as strong and caring, willing to do anything to help another human being. Yet when they finally realize that the hurt inside of them is too much to carry, no one else seems to notice. Hearts that are hurt or broken don't bleed, which is why most people don't see their pain until the pain takes over their life and allows itself to be seen.

Yet what we see isn't a physical injury of bleeding or broken bones; what we see is a fallen angel with its' soul bruised and its' wings broken. They fell because they loved and cared more for others than they did for themselves. When they fall, those around them begin to judge them unfairly. No one sees the real injury; they only see the problem that the brokenness has caused. They see the mistakes, yet not the truths. They see a burden, rather than a blessing. You see, the fallen angel doesn't fall because they chose to; they fall because they were chosen.

They were chosen to learn from falling, because they are the ones chosen for greatness. They are the ones that are strong enough to feel the pain, fall, and get back up, no matter how long it takes.

They are the ones that will always love and help others, yet they will learn through the fall how to love themselves first.

They were chosen to fall because a Higher Power had a plan for them and trusted them enough to know that the fall wouldn't break them. Instead, the fall would build them stronger. This new strength they found would eventually change the world of another fallen angel.

Fallen Angels are not weak; on the contrary, they are stronger than most people I know. They are the ones that had to go through hell to get to heaven, and whether most think that's lucky or not, I believe that going through hell can be lucky. It's through that experience that they've seen the difference, and not many of us get that chance.

Fallen angels are the hope and the faith that there is something bigger and greater than us; and if you want to experience a miracle here on Earth, watch a fallen angel get its' wings back and fly!

"Grief Stricken"

Grief: an unimaginable pain that's embedded into your heart. It comes without warning and doesn't easily dissipate; it's an emotion that comes from losing someone you had loved and still love. There are many other emotions you live with during a lifetime, yet grief seems to be the only one that forms a bond within your heart that no amount of medication or therapy can seem to break.

Is that because we won't allow the bond to be broken or that it truly can't be broken?

What is grief?

It's an overwhelming emotion caused by the loss of someone we love, whether by the loss of a child, a parent or loved one; it's the end of a relationship as we knew it on earth, and it transcends past the physical world into the spiritual world.

So many people who haven't experienced it simply tell the "grief stricken" that they'll get through it, or at its' worst, will tell them they grieved long enough. Yet they don't know and can't understand that this isn't a broken heart to be healed. It's a broken piece of your soul. Broken hearts heal; broken souls simply mend and have to adjust to living life differently.

Time doesn't heal grief; it simply allows the grief to find its place among the living.

My belief is that grief is the eternal love the soul on this Earth has for the soul that has passed on, around and through us. The soul of those lost take up permanent residence in our heart, and our "grief" process is to learn to tuck them in tightly, so as to escape the comments of those who have one.

Yet grief is not an emotion to hide, nor should it be. It is the confirmation that someone was loved so deeply and unconditionally that souls had been connected in a way that no other has, and that connection cannot and will not be broken.

And why should it?

For those grieving, it's the only way to hold on and hold it within. It's that place they go to be with the soul they lost. It's a comfort zone, filled with warmth and love, pain and suffering, yet it's the one place that holds their loved one close within them.

My question is this: "Are these people grief stricken or grief living?" I believe the answer is that they're one in the same.

There are those that go to psychics and mediums to get in touch with their loved one, yet what they don't realize is while that may be one approach, they were given the power to connect with them at the moment their loved one crossed. They just don't realize that until they are willing to.

Lost souls live among us and within us. You can find them, whether sleeping or awake, by simply calling for them. It's then that we can truly connect with and find them. We may hear them, smell their essence or feel their presence. It may frighten us to know that we have that ability, and it's that fear that may hold them back from us connecting, yet in time you will be able to connect with them.

Yet know this: no connection bound with love is ever broken or ever lost. It lives on forever, because it was formed with the greatest of emotions: unconditional love. True love can never be broken, or is ever truly lost. The physical aspect of a touch or hug may be gone, but the soul connection of comfort and love can never be lost.

It can seem as if it's lost because those grieving may feel lost; and for some, they are. How do you escape a feeling that you weren't prepared for? How do you move on from something that you never intended to move towards?

You do it, one day, one breath, and one moment at a time. You dismiss the fear of losing the connection with their soul, and embrace the faith that they will never leave you; their physical body may leave, yet their soul never does.

Trust the journey, as life is ever changing. What we have today could be gone in moments. Embrace each day you wake up and take a breath; love those around you with a passion; and keep those you lost close within your heart.

And if you ever need that connection and want to feel their spirit, just sit quietly, close your eyes, and call on them. Remember, they loved you as much as you loved them.

Take a breath, and breathe them into your body and soul…and they will breathe in the life force of your own being. Find them inside and outside of you; they're waiting for you to call to them as much as you're waiting for them to come to you.

"Under the Tree"

There's a quiet spot right under the tree
Where the messages of loved ones come to me.
They're the voices I remember of those who have passed
Their love and their light, the sound of their laugh.
I don't grieve of their passing, I don't cry bitter tears
I smile with a joy at the voices I hear.
Friends and family, lost babies and such
My heart's very full having loved them so much.
The love never dies, only the shell of their soul
Their spirit lives inside me; it's my heart that they hold.
I know I can't touch them, no hug and no kiss
Yet a thought brings them back, only their body to miss.
For each single memory, for every sweet thought
They remind me of their life and the happiness it brought.
All I need to remember, all I need to see
Can be found in the silence while sitting under the tree.

~Anne Dennish~

"A Letter to My Children"

I remember each and every birth of all of you, and not one was the same. You slid from within me to outside of me in a mere push, and suddenly, you were born; you were granted the gift of life, of your life. And on the day the first of you was born, I was re-born. I was no longer just a married woman; I was born again as a mother. Life changed from that exact moment that you took your first breath, and with that breath, I held mine. I held my breath out of excitement of a new baby placed in my arms, and out of fear as to all the responsibilities that were now a part of my life, from that day forward. I was fearful that I would make a mistake in caring for you, in raising you; I was fearful of this new woman I had become, because within that moment that you travelled from within me, I realized for the first time what "love" really was, and it was so deep, so strong, that it felt as though my heart would burst. And the fear of who I would become without you swept throughout my body, and was as foreign a concept to me as being pregnant for the first time and feeling another human inside of me kick. What would happen to me if anything happened to you? Your birth was the best dream I ever had, with all the feelings of a nightmare wrapped up inside of it. You, my children, were my dreams all come true, yet with each one of you came the nightmare of hoping you'd always be okay, that you'd never get hurt, that your life would be without any feelings of low self esteem, or anger, or sadness that I had ever felt. I never wanted you to feel anything less than joy, yet as a mother, I knew I couldn't protect you from the world as you grew older. I could teach you how to protect yourselves, yet I knew that I could never protect your heart from hurting from others. I could kiss you, hug you, and tell you lots of deceptions to make you feel better, but I wouldn't be able to stop the outside world from coming in.

Mother's aren't perfect; we only seem that way until you get a bit older and realize we're not. Mothers don't hurt their children's heart, yet it happens, unintentionally and without malice. You, my children, forget that just as you were born not knowing the outside world yet, I was born not knowing the inside of the world I had now entered…motherhood. I know this for fact, and it's hard to admit, that unless we admit our mistakes, we never learn from them. I hope I have taught you that because I have learned that from all of you. There is no perfect mother, or father, or child; what there is are all of us striving and working at being the best person we can be that day. Some days we fall short, but are always blessed with another new day to do it better, with no mistakes in it. Life, my children, is not meant to be lived in perfection, but to be embraced with love for the mistakes we make, and the sincerity of making it better when we make them. Without mistakes, unintentional mistakes to be exact, we never learn. We may be hurt by

WAKING UP

them, yet they are instrumental teachers on our journey of becoming the mother we are, and the adults you become.

The love of a mother never dies, not with time, not with distance, not with death; the love of a mother grows stronger with each passing day; with each new milestone you reach and each heartache you encounter. Your mistakes become lessons for us, and with each mistake, together we become stronger, and better for it.

There is nothing that can or will break or lessen the love a mother has for her children; the heart of a mother is the heart of her child.

And you, my child, are forever and always within and around my heart.

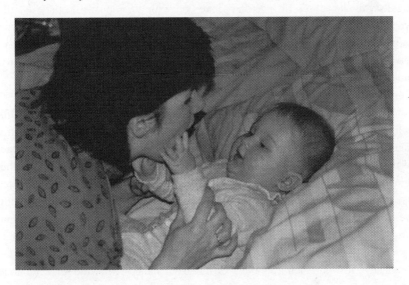

"Ruthless People"

Our children can be the most ruthless people on the face of the earth. They are the ones that can fill out heart with so much joy and happiness that we feel like we're in heaven; it's a feeling of love that we never knew before.

They are also the ones that can break your heart in a million pieces with their lack of forgiveness for our imperfections that we never claimed NOT to have in the first place; it's a feeling of despair, hurt, and sadness like we never knew before.

And that's what makes them ruthless. "It's all fun and games until someone gets hurt" is an old saying with a much different meaning, yet when your child breaks your heart, it's fitting. They love you with abandon while they're little; we're perfect to them and know how to fix every wound, every sorrow, every sadness; we are as smart as a genius to them, and they believe every answer we tell them. There is undying trust, and undying love… until they begin to grow older and mature.

Suddenly we're not perfect, and every word out of our mouth, every action we perform, every joke we tell becomes "stupid" and suddenly, there is no smiling face looking at us like they used to; now it's a face with eyes rolling into the back of their heads. They don't believe us, don't trust us, and certainly act as if they don't love us. Sometimes they even act as though they don't even know us! We used to know all their dreams, their hopes, their secrets, yet now we know nothing; we're living in a home with our child whose life we're not welcome in, and they are sure to let us know that. See, it was all fun and games for them, until we got hurt.

They grow into their 20's and 30's, move out and move on, and forget all about us…at least until they remember they need us.

I don't remember when they were younger and teaching them "please" and "thank you" that I ever threw in "Mommy and Daddy are perfect; Mommy and Daddy never make mistakes." Yet somehow, in between the alphabet and Dr. Seuss, amidst coloring in the lines to learning a new language, they believed that we taught them that. And they never forgot it. They may have forgotten to take out the trash, do their homework, and that they had a curfew, but they never forget something we never told them: I am perfect. I make no mistakes.

And that's where they become ruthless, because while it's not our fault they believe something we never taught them, rather than what we did, they will take us to task, bring us to our knees, hold a hearing in which they are the jury...and many times there is no leniency, parole, or forgiveness; simply a sentence. And the sentence can be long, from a few days, to a few months, to a few years, and the worst of all, a lifetime.

We always forgave our kids when they made mistakes, because we loved them and knew they would make mistakes, yet why weren't we given the same courtesy and respect. Is it because we're older; or their parents; or simply because they can?

It's because we are the parents and they are the children, and while there are no definitive rules where this is concerned, there is the proverbial knowing that they are not here to love us; we are here to love them.

"Preach It, Teach It...Then Reach for It"

Every morning at around 5 am, I sit outside with my coffee in silence. I listen to the sounds that seem to be heard only at this quiet, peaceful time of day. It's my "sacred space" when the kids are still asleep and the phone doesn't ring. It's that first cup of coffee that I enjoy with no interruptions. It is truly my "magical" time of day before the daily routine of home, kids, and work begins. I'm more creative, more focused, and for me, the most important thing that happens during this time is this: I can hear. I can hear my thoughts, my heart, my dreams, and suddenly this quiet time is filled with my inner voice, my intuition, which I believe to be God and my Angels speaking to me. Call it what you will, but I know this is the one time of day I receive the answers to my questions.

As I sat here this morning, the thoughts began pouring in about my goals in life, my dreams and how quickly everything in my life is changing, all for the good. Yet there are still pieces of myself that need work, people that still need to be out of my life, and change that still needs to happen.

People will often tell me that I'm an "inspiration," that I have a gift of words that touches them. Some have said I seem to write something that suddenly is the answer to their questions. Yet as I sit this morning pondering all of this, I realize that to some extent they're right. I give great advice when asked, and have a gift to see them and be able to help them with whatever they need help with. Then there's "me." I can teach it through writing, preach it through words, yet I need to learn to "reach" for it for me.

I believe that all dreams can come true if you have the faith and the drive to "go for it." I live my own life that way, and have taught my children that all dreams are possible if you want it bad enough. I have proudly sat back and watched my children take a dream or two and make it become a reality. I gave them the tools to do this; they did the work to get it.

Yet I know personally, there are things in my life today that are not for my highest good, and unless they are changed, my dreams will take longer, or may not happen at all; the goals will be met but not as soon as I'd hoped; that today I am healthy but unless I change some of my behaviors, that may change tomorrow.

I sat and beat myself up for a few moments, and thought to myself: "if you want all good things for those you know, those you love, those you just meet, why don't you want that for yourself? "The answer is simple: I do. The problem is that

WAKING UP

I tend to get caught up in every other aspect of life that I forget to pay attention to myself. I forget to balance my mind, body and spirit, and only remember to do so when I'm exhausted, or don't feel well. It's when that happens that I'm forced to stop what I'm doing and rest...and think about why it happened. It's then I realize that while I'm busy with the house, the kids, the work, and helping others, I remember, yet again, that I forgot to put "me" first. I forgot to take care of all of those things in me that I know are the essence of being able to do what I love, take care of those I care about, and function through the daily routines of my own life. Yes, it's a slap in the face, but a necessary one, as it reminds me to do what I preach to everyone else to do.

So on this beautiful morning, as the sun is about to rise, the voices inside of my head remind me that I am loved, I am love, and that it's "ok" to forget every so often, as long as I "remember." This morning I remembered. I remembered about "me."

I watch so many people fall into the pattern I tend to fall into every so often, and while I can teach it and preach it to them, I have to consistently "reach" for it for myself. We lead by example, we teach by example, and all the preaching in the world will never change what we can't do ourselves.

I embrace moments like this morning when I realize where I've fallen short. I know it doesn't happen often, yet it happens. It's nothing to beat myself up over, as I'm as human as the next person. Yet I embrace it as another moment to "teach" myself to remember, and my intuition I hear is "preaching" to me. Another moment of clarity, another defining moment in my life of what I forgot, what I need to remember, and what I need to do.

Loving oneself isn't selfish, it's selfless, because all these wonderful gifts I have are then passed to those around me, and before you know it, all of them are being found in them. My happiness, my joy, my balance will have an effect on the people I come in contact with everyday, be it my children, a stranger, or a friend on the phone.

I'm thankful this morning for being reminded of what I forgot, of knowing what I need to do for myself, and for being reassured that I am loved, flaws and all, forgetful or not, and so are all of you. You are loved, you are love, and are worthy of all good things in life.

I'll teach it and preach it to you; now **YOU** need to go out and reach for it!

"Caution: You're About to Make a Memory"

Memories: we've all got them, good ones and bad. Every day is another opportunity to make a memory, so proceed with caution: the memory you make today can easily turn into the bad memory of your future. Once again, it's that old perception theory: "it's all about how you look at things."

Memories are captured in a million different ways: pictures, heirlooms, saved reminders of the past, love notes and more, yet the memories that stick with us for a lifetime are the memories in which our "heart takes a picture."

Those are my favorite memories; the ones that make you stop in the middle of the day and smile, remembering the feelings from that exact moment your heart took that picture. We smile with joy from the memory, and sadness at the loss of it.

Memories aren't made only of the "big" moments in life, they are born of those sweet, precious, small moments that are a miracle in itself; your child's first laugh, the feeling of falling in love, the excitement of being promoted at work, or the realization that you just caught one of your dreams. They can be big or small, lasting a moment or a lifetime. The moment may not last, yet the memory will last for a lifetime.

So why do I say "caution?" It's because as others makes memories for "us," we also are making memories for "them." The last thing you want to do is leave someone's mind with a bad memory. There are times a bad memory can't be helped; it's life at its best and worst, and it's all in how you perceive it.

My marriage lasted 20 years, and while there were many wonderful memories, there were painful ones as well. Yet through the years, I've learned to forgive the bad ones, tuck them away, and look at them only when I need to be reminded of what I had learned from them. I've learned that while I may wish the bad stuff didn't happen, I'll never regret that it did. It was meant to, and with that way of thinking, I get through it, around it and over it all.

"When you can't get over something, go around it!"

Sounds easy, doesn't it?

It's not.

Not by a long shot…

but you can do it;

with time and effort;

and by learning how to love yourself.

That's how it's done. You need to love yourself and know who you are so that you can accept that it had to happen, was meant to happen, and will continue to happen if you haven't learned the lesson from the experience.

We keep repeating the same patterns and making the same memories until we learn and make the effort to allow ourselves to grow into the best person we can be. You want a better job, marriage or relationship? Then take stock of your past for a brief moment, accept what it was meant to teach you, and carry the lessons tucked in your heart.

> *"Sometimes we have to revisit our past to remind us of why we left it behind in the first place."*

You can visit the past, but don't stay too long. When you're feeling out of sorts, or wondering why the same scenarios keep happening in your life, then take those few moments of going back in time. Stay only long enough to remember why you left it there in the first place. Grab your lesson like you'd grab the brass ring on a merry go round and move on. Carry it within you, not all over you. Allow it to embed that lesson inside of you. Let it be a memory; a gift that brought you back to yourself and helped you to grow. Let it be a precious memory that enabled you to be where you are today: happy!

Memories are lasting impressions others make on us and we on them. That last look, that last conversation or phone call, can easily become a memory. Choose your thoughts, your actions, your words and your intentions carefully because once that memory is out there, it's there for a lifetime.

Adjust it if you have the chance, alter it you can, and forgive yourself if you can't.

Just as we have control over the memories others' have given us, they have the same control over the ones' we've given them. You may be in a place to perceive their memories in a kinder, gentler way, yet they may not be. That is where you need to proceed with caution.

Once words are out there, they can't be taken back. They can be forgiven, but they're never forgotten. They last like a cloud of negativity, and can come back to haunt us at any given moment.

That's the funny thing with memories, they truly do last a lifetime. They can change over time, get more dramatic or intense, or become calmer and less of what they originally were, but they are there.

Box up the memories that no longer serve you and revisit your past only when you need to. Make your life a box of amazing memories, for yourself and for those around you.

Let your "heart take a picture." Make some incredible memories!

"I Wish I Had Never..."

If I had a nickel for every time I've said "I wish I had never," I'd be a rich woman, yet then again, through all the experiences on my journey of life, I've learned not to say it as often. While I may have been a rich woman counting my nickels, I'm richer now by counting my silver dollars. I've learned never to wish my mistakes or bad experiences away, because they made me who I am today, and the ones to come will make me who I am in the future.

We all look back at times on the mistakes we made, the heartache we endured, the physical pain we conquered, and for a brief moment, wish it had never happened. Yet once we return back to our sanity, we understand and accept that it all **HAD** to happen. In the end, everything turned out alright; it may not have been what we were hoping for, yet it landed us right where we needed to be.

"Life sometimes takes us on an unexpected journey;

we may not end up where we dreamed,

but we'll always end up where we belong."

I believe those words with all my heart, based on my years of experience. There were times I wished:

- that I had never gone back to someone who cheated on me
- that I never gave a second chance to someone that never deserved one
- that I never allowed someone to treat me with less respect than I gave
- that I had taken better care of myself
- that I had said "I love you" to someone sooner
- that I had been a better mother
- that I had been a better wife
- that I had started catching my dreams years ago

- that I hadn't waited so long to understand who I am

You see that list of "I wish I had never?" Well, there's an answer to each of them and reasons to why I no longer wish that:

- the cheater taught me to place a higher value on myself

- the second chance taught me that sometimes we need to go back to understand why we left in the first place

- that not being respected by someone else taught me that I must first respect myself in order for anyone else to

- that having breast cancer taught me to take better care of myself, which would enable me to care for those around me

- that every day is precious, and it's important to let the people you care about and love know how feel

- that I was the best mother I knew how to be, that not being perfect was human, and that any mistake was made out of love, not anger

- that it takes two people to break a marriage, and I was the best wife I could be to the man I was married to

- that being a stay at home mom was important during that time, and at the time, being a mother was my dream

- that I've been learning about myself all along, except as I grow older, I pay more attention to the lessons.

You see, for everything I used to wish never happened, I don't regret that they did. They happened for a reason. They made me who I am today, and while I'm not perfect, I love, respect and appreciate who I am. All those experiences helped me to learn more about myself, and honestly, that's how I've come to know myself so well. I've learned to change my perspective on life, to stop wasting my precious time on the "wishes" and focus on the "dreams." I've learned to accept all things that happen along my journey as learning experiences. I know there will still be times I forget the lesson and a similar situation will arise, yet it takes less time to see it now. There are no mistakes, just experiences.

WAKING UP

Don't waste your energy on the "wishes of the past." Focus your energy on the dreams of today, the dreams of tomorrow, and the dreams you hold deep within your heart. Accept that your "less than perfect" days are just a day, and it won't be like that forever. Life is a choice, love is a choice, and living is a choice. Choose wisely and you'll never again have a moment of "I wish that never happened." It happened to help you, heal you, and teach you. And isn't that why we're all here?

"The Voice of the Ocean"

I'm a true Jersey girl, born and raised at the Jersey Shore, living only five minutes from the beach. Yet as I write this, I'm sitting in a friends' Malibu beach house, the waves crashing under the house at high tide, leaving a beach to walk on during low tide. As I sit on the deck, watching the waves crashing, smelling the salt air, and listening to the sounds of the ocean and all the creatures flying above, I'm suddenly hearing more than that. I'm hearing the voice of the ocean, which is filled with messages and thought provoking questions.

I came out here for the solitude and peace to write so that I could finish this book that has taken me far too long to write at home; a home filled with kids, my significant other, two dogs and a cat, and of course, bills, laundry, cooking and cleaning. This was an opportunity to write and to be alone. Yet a mission to write became much more during this trip; it became one of soul searching as well. For those who know me, and for those who read this book, I'm constantly watching and listening, because that is how my stories are born.

They are born out of lessons in life, be it mine or someone else's, through observing situations and people, and more importantly, they are born out of listening to my intuition, hearing what my inner thoughts are saying, and finding the answers to my own questions.

Of all the places I've been in this world, nothing speaks louder to me than the ocean. It has a voice all its' own; a peaceful rhythm not found anywhere else. It doesn't take a break, is constantly in motion, and changes throughout the day and night. No two pictures of it are alike. Yet when you're alone to do nothing but sit and stare at the wonder and miracle of it, your mind begins to wander. It wanders to familiar places, such as life back home, and wanders to unfamiliar places, such as pondering what your life purpose is, why did you come here, and more importantly for me: what are you doing with your life?

The voice of the ocean is speaking loudly and clearly to me more today than the last few. It took some time to settle in to a home not my own, to find my comfort zone, to feel at ease. Yet now that I've found that peace, the ocean is talking... and it's talking a lot; and it's forced me to listen.

My life has changed so much in the last few years, and even few months. I survived chemo, surgery and breast cancer, a bad break-up, leaving a job, saying good bye to family that weren't family at all, and lived through another child moving out of the nest. Yet while there were some losses, there were gains: I fell in love, I started a small business, I gained a few friends that became family to me, and I've found myself writing in the world of racing. I'd say that proves my theory of "everything happens for a reason," and sometimes the hardest changes in our life are worth the effort to allow better things to come.

Yet here I am, listening to my new best friend, the ocean, speak to me in a way it never has before, and for the first time in my life, things are making sense, and pieces of the puzzle of my life that were missing for years are suddenly finding their place.

When you sit in silence long enough, allowing only the sounds of the sea to fill your mind, you'll soon hear all the answers to questions you may have never known you had.

This is what I hear:

That I loved more than I allowed myself to be loved; that because I've not given someone else a chance to prove that they can love me as well as I can love them, I couldn't feel it. I feel it now.

That my feeling that I was lost and had forgotten "who" I was happened because of me; I shut myself down, and placed more importance on those around me than on myself. I may not have thought I was doing that, and may have had a million excuses why it happened, yet the truth is that I allowed it to happen. The truth is I didn't want to face my own truth, or lack of it. Now I do.

That those moments of listening to someone who was hurtful to me made me feel bad; feel like I was a failure; feel that all my dreams were as stupid as they had always made me to believe they were. I know now that I have always allowed them that power and control over me, and these feelings of "questioning whether I was good enough or not" were my own fault. Only I can control how I feel about myself, and no matter who puts me down or hurts me, I allowed it. I know now how to stay in control.

That feeling scared is losing sight of my faith; not all situations, such as cancer, can be stopped, but with the right attitude, anything is possible, and the journey of getting through anything life hands us is best done with a positive attitude and faith. Faith that it happened for a reason; the knowledge that my Higher Power didn't do it to me on purpose, yet is there to see me

through it; trust in myself and my intuition, because when I'm in tune with my inner voice, I can hear.

That God truly lives in me, as I am a child of God, and no matter how many people will love me in this world, His is a constant love, one more imaginable that we can perceive; it never lessens and it never ends. If I could love myself in even the smallest ways that God does, I'll be just fine. And I'm learning to do just that.

That loyalty is one of the most important qualities in any situation we're in; without it, there's no trust, no compassion, no remorse. Lack of loyalty is nothing short of lies to make you believe something that isn't really there. I've learned to see the difference.

That having been broken many times doesn't mean I can't be healed. I was broken because I lost sight of myself; I forgot that I need to love and respect myself first in order to have anyone love and respect me. I was broken to learn, and healed to make a difference to someone else. As long as I learned that loving myself first was crucial, the broken can be healed, and stronger than not. I know now just how strong I am.

I sit now, listening to the voice of the ocean as it quiets down, allowing only the sounds of the breaking waves to be heard. I realize that the ocean is an example of what we should strive to be: constant, strong, and ever changing. No two waves are alike, just as no two human beings are either, yet the ocean lives within itself with all those differences, and as far as I can tell, it hasn't missed a day of wonderment or a moment of being miraculous yet. Why should we be any less?

"Beliefs"

Everyone believes in something, in fact, we believe in many things. It's our belief in what we know today, not of yesterday or of tomorrow, just today. It's all the things that we've learned in our life up until this point that gives us a list of things we know to be true, which I call our "beliefs." Ask anyone this question: What do you believe in? You'll find a variety of answers. Some answers may be negative or positive, optimistic or pessimistic, cynical or dreamy. Yet what's fascinating to me is that each of our beliefs are based on all the experiences we've lived through up until this very day: today. They're not good or bad, wrong or right, they just "are."

I believe that:

- All people have goodness in them, yet it's their choice to express it, or suppress it.

- We have a choice every day to be happy or sad.

- Our children can break our hearts unlike anyone else.

- Some people lie.

- Loyalty is a forgotten word.

- Love means something different to all of us, and the best relationships are founded on finding someone whose definition of love is most similar to ours.

- Sex is simply a perk in a relationship; friendship, respect, and compassion are what make the best relationship.

- Everything happens for a reason.

- Every "not so good" thing that happens to us will eventually lead us to "something wonderful."

- We can't expect everyone to treat us as good as we treat them; "expect nothing and you'll never be disappointed."

- There are people that don't deserve second chances; when someone shows you their true colors, believe them and move on.

- We need to see people for whom they are "today," not for the potential of who they may become with time.

- Cutting people out of your life doesn't mean you don't care about them or love them; it just means you love yourself more.

- Stress can wreak havoc on your body and your mind.

- You should only trust someone when they have earned it.

- The people you believe will never hurt you are actually the ones who will hurt you the most.

- Life is black and white; right and wrong. There are no gray areas, which in reality is simply a way of justifying wrong behavior.

- You should only say you're sorry if you're willing to change the behavior that made you say it in the first place.

- You should never say anything you don't mean in anger, nor should someone say it to you; words spoken out loud live on in our memory for a lifetime. You may forgive it, but you'll never forget it.

- Everything is forgivable, just not always repairable.

- Bringing up the past only stops the future from moving forward.

- If someone treats you badly, it's because you allowed it.

- Never say "I don't have a choice" because you have one every single day in every single situation you're in.

- Broken hearts will mend, but they never mend the same as before they were broken. They'll mend stronger.

- You can't change anyone, and no matter how wonderful you are, it's up to them to change if they want to.

WAKING UP

- A long, hot lavender sea salt bath cures anything and will help you sleep.

- Our dreams hold more of the answers to our questions than our waking moments.

- God is real, and Angels are always surrounding us.

- Everything and anything is always possible.

- You can manifest the life you want.

- Every single thing in life means something.

- Everyone has a story if you take the time to listen.

- Intuition is God speaking to us; and if we don't listen, not much goes the way we want.

- Mercury in Retrograde is real.

- "Using your voice" in a kind, yet strong tone, has the ability to change your life.

- We meet every single person for a reason.

- Angels come in all shapes and forms; these are the "Earth Angels."

- Music and dancing can change a mood and it's good for the soul.

- No one should have to explain themselves to anyone; too much explaining gives someone else the control.

- Domestic violence is all the same; getting hit with a hand hurts just as much as being punched with words. Bruises go away; hurtful words do not.

- I am in control of my life.

- You have to let go of your past in order for your present and future to have a chance at being all that it can.

- Nothing should define us; we define ourselves.

- Love doesn't stand a chance without trust.

- Sometimes what we've believed to be true turns out to not have been true at all.

- Letting go is the only way to move forward.

- When we thought we were loved by someone we were only filling an empty space in their world, not their heart.

- Loving someone enough to let them go is the most self-less thing we can do.

- Loving our self the way we want someone to love us is the only way we'll find a love that is real.

My beliefs may change over time, or through the lessons learned from situations, yet the "belief" is and will always be the most important one:

"I believe in me."

Lessons Learned Through My Adventures with Breast Cancer

My personal journal entries

"A Note from the Author"

The chapters you are about to read are from the journal I kept throughout my adventures with breast cancer. They aren't edited, as I wanted to share them with you exactly as I had written them at the time. Life with breast cancer wasn't perfect, and neither are the entries from my journal, yet I hope that as you read them it will help you or someone else going through this battle, or any other battle for that fact.

My battle with breast cancer is over, and I am much more diligent in caring for my body, mind and soul. If it took cancer to teach me that, it was well worth it. My hope is that my battle will not become someone else's, because while breast cancer isn't preventable, you can catch it early, and that's the key.

As of today, I am cancer free and about to hit another anniversary. My wish and prayer for all of you going through this disease is for you to be as fortunate as I was, and that you will be celebrating your anniversaries as well.

Wishing love and light to all of you!

~Anne Dennish~

"A Bump in the Road to My Happiness...Day One"

July 13, 2013

    I always write about uplifting things in my life, hoping that my experiences will touch someone who needs touching into believing that everything happens for a reason, and that happiness is our choice. So far, my stories are one of helping others, sending out positive energy of love and light to all those who take the time to read them. As I sit here writing this, the strong, courageous, fearless, upbeat, positive, happy woman everyone knows me to be doesn't exist today. Today I'm feeling scared and nervous of the unknown, trying to find the reason for "this."

    I've been so happy lately, filled with a peace like I've not known in a long time. I accept everything that comes my way as just another step along my journey in life. I seem to have more of an understanding of those I care about and love, and am diligently chasing my dreams that make me so happy. Last night was the "bump," or you could say, the "lump" on the road to my happiness.

    As I lie in bed last night with someone I care about, his hand was on my breast, and suddenly it felt like a breast exam. He stopped dead in his tracks at one point and asked me what "this" was, and did I know it was there? I felt it, and no, I had never felt it before, and no, it had never been there before. He asked me not to wait on getting this checked out and I agreed. I fell asleep for a while, and woke up to the thoughts of this proverbial "bump on the road to my happiness." I hated to leave him there, but knew I had to leave. At that moment, I didn't know where I needed to be. My only option was to go home.

    I got home and the tears flowed like a faucet on full force; alone and no one to talk to. Yet, there is one person, my best "guy" friend who lives thousands of miles away: Theo. He's the only person I know that I can call any time of day or night that will answer my call and listen. Last night was no exception. I called him well after midnight and he answered, and more importantly, he let me cry my eyes out over how scared I was, how I didn't want to die, and that the worst part of all this was I'd have to go through it alone. I'm a single mom with four kids living home. How does the parent who does it all for them get sick and still take care of them? I never felt more alone in my life, and if this is a test of my strength, my intention is to win. I've lived through some incredibly awful things in my life, always keeping the faith and staying strong, yet this feels different. I'm alone, and just like the lump that's in my breast, that's a fact.

Theo's advice to me was to keep a journal about all of this, and that it might not be a bad idea to let everyone share in my experience. So, here's my first journal entry on my "bump on the road to my happiness." I saw the doctor today, and I could tell by the tone of her voice and the look of concern on her face that it doesn't look good. I searched throughout the internet all night long and I know what all the signs point to. This lump is large, hard, and not moving. This may turn out to be nothing, a little something, or a lot of something. The waiting game sucks right about now, especially for those who know me as the "need to know" girl that I am. Well, I'm not going to get all the answers today, or even in the next few days. I always consider myself to be one of the most patient people in the world, yet my patience is about to be tested in a way I've never known before.

I realized something very important at the doctor's office today. I may be strong and can handle anything, yet throughout the last few years I lost sight of being strong for myself by not taking care of myself. I should have been smarter and known better, and yes, I'm kicking myself for that today. Yet, it's here and I can't change it. I can only change it from this day forward.

Today I want to sleep, but I can't; I want to talk, but I don't; I want to run, but there's no place to go. There's no arms outstretched to hold me through this, only voices on the phone. I appreciate the voices, but for today, I would welcome the arms. Perhaps this happened to this writer, this "word girl" for a reason. Maybe, just maybe, there's someone who needs to learn from my "mistake" of not paying enough attention to my health and my body. All of that changed this morning.

There's always a reason, yet not always an answer. Today I feel the sadness, feel the fear. Tomorrow I'll wake up and kick ass, just like every other day. Being strong is all that I know, and in the next few days, I'm about to know a lot more. Welcome to yet another journey in my life and this "bump on the road to my happiness."

"A Bump on the Road to My Happiness... Day Two"

July 14, 2013

I decided to drink it away last night, so I did. I fell asleep around 2am and woke up at 6am, and guess what? The lump was still there. Damn, I thought I'd drink that and all the feelings that went with it away. It didn't work.

My first thought was one of being very pissed off. How could all these people, these "friends" that I'm always there for suddenly become non-existent? How dare they go on with their normal, fun lives when I felt like mine had just been stopped dead in its tracks? I know it makes no sense to feel that way, and I'm not one to be angry at anyone for anything. I don't judge anyone's behavior, or lack of, and suddenly I found myself doing just that. I knew it wasn't fair, I knew it wasn't me, but I haven't been "me" since Friday night. It was then I decided to give myself permission to "not" be me, because this was a much different circumstance than normal. I hoped that my friends would be as understanding of my behavior as I was trying to be.

My second thought was: "how do I keep someone from being as stupid as I was?" My answer is to keep going with my journal.

I had a vision last night of exactly how I believe this will go: I go for the tests, have the lump aspirated, and because of my age, have a lumpectomy which turns out to be benign. I can live with that; this is my wake up call. What I'm not sure I can live with is a scar to remind me every day for the rest of my life how stupid I was. I know it all sounds crazy, and I should be happy when it turns out to be "no cancer." Trust me, I'll be grateful if it does, but for now, "forgive me" for all the feelings that I'm going through right now.

I'm not stressing, not very worried; I'm just scared, and I was so hoping there'd be someone on the other end of the phone or in person that would realize I just need to talk, to get out for some fun. I needed someone to do anything it took to get my mind off it. There was no one.

Of course I'm afraid to have cancer, but I'm more afraid of all those people I've loved and cared about, whom I've been a great friend to, dropping out of my life. Life is going to change, true colors of those I care for are about to come out like the colors of a rainbow after a storm.

"A Bump on the Road to My Happiness… Day Three"

July 18, 2013

Today I need to get an appointment for my mammogram and ultrasound. I started calling places at 7 am, and the earliest appointments I could get would mean waiting a week. I couldn't wait, and I'm sure most women couldn't. I set my intention in my mind that I would find the best place and have an appointment today. By 10am I had one scheduled for 1pm.

I drove to the hospital, and was sent directly to the Women's Clinic. I wasn't worried after the first mammogram, or the second. As the afternoon wore on, however, I lost count after having six of them. I knew this couldn't be good. I finally met the doctor, a wonderful woman who I trusted with my life, so to speak, the moment I met her. She spent quite some time doing my ultrasound. The first small tear fell when she told me to meet me in her office followed with "Do you have someone to drive you home?" I knew right there that I was not about to hear that everything was fine.

We met in the office, and as she began speaking I continued to write everything down. I could hear her voice, but nothing seemed to be registering in my brain. **"18mm tumor, and three, possibly four other masses that were not normal and cause for concern."** The tears came, and once they started, they wouldn't stop. The doctor said she wanted to treat this aggressively and not wait. She wanted to do four needle biopsies on Thursday. I left the hospital after being there over six hours, and got into my car.

I called my best friend, Colleen, and sobbed my heart out on the phone. She told me to just sit in the car and not drive until I could calm down. So I sat in the car, in 90 degree heat for twenty minutes, crying, talking and listening to her. Colleen will come up on Thursday to take me for the biopsy, and being the nurse she is, she'll ask all the right questions that I might not be able to.

I drove home, crying most of the trip, made two or three phone calls, and told my children. I didn't cry in front of them, I kept it light, and tried to infuse as much laughter and joking into this conversation as I could. They know I'm strong, they know I'll be fine…I also know how scared they are.

And so the journey continues…

"Biopsy Day for the Bump in My Road to Happiness"

July 18, 2013

The day is here: biopsy at 2pm. I thank God for Colleen wanting to drive all the way from Delaware to be with me. I'm not really sure what my emotions are at the moment. A few tears fell this morning, but I pushed them aside and decided to just be my cheerful, perky, positive, upbeat self! It's working most of the time, but I'll admit, not all the time. The oncologist liaison told me the emotions will be all over the place at times; that it's normal, and I should expect them to be worse after the biopsy because I'll have a whole weekend to go through of waiting and wondering. I already knew that. Looks like it might be a great weekend to get out, get away, drink a lot of wine, and listen to great music! Yet the reality is that no matter what I do, it's on my mind and in my body.

The amazing thing to me is how many people have seen this journal without my even posting it on social media. I've received some beautiful emails from people I haven't spoken to in years, and what a blessing that is! See, my mantra on life is that "out of everything bad something wonderful will happen." This still rings true, and no cancer will change that. I may give in to the crappy emotions of fear and anger that come with this on occasion, but it won't last long. That's not me.

I've been writing all morning, doing social media pages for my business, and answering a few phone calls from my friends. Life goes on, and it will. At this very moment, I'm thinking positive, feeling blessed for everything and everyone, and ready to start another phase on this journey of my life.

I have cancer, and that's hard to say, especially when the few people who I've told don't believe it to be true. I will be fine, yet it's getting from this point to "fine" that scares me a bit. I have faith, and I know God and all my wonderful Angels are watching over me.

Welcome to my journey, thank you for sharing it with me, and please let my lesson be your blessing to take care of yourself. "Life is what happens to you while you're busy making other plans." Don't ever get that busy again…I know this to be true.

"Biopsy... Done!"

July 19, 2013

Colleen picked me up for my biopsy this afternoon, and before I knew it, we were on our way. I signed in, and we sat there, joking it all off as well as we could. The joking stopped when they told me who my surgeon was. Surgeon? When did that happen? Then, it was time. Biopsy #1: I laid face down on the table for 45 minutes, with about 5 samples taken. I have to say, it hurt. The lanacaine to numb the area was no picnic, and neither was the biopsy. I lay there, one arm above my head, for about 45 minutes, my thoughts wandering from here to there. When it was over, it was back out to the waiting room with Colleen. A few minutes later, the ultrasound biopsy. This one was on my back and I asked if I could watch it. The doctor said I could if I really wanted to, but didn't suggest it. Well, I opted to watch the whole thing.

There it was on the screen, that damn tumor. I wanted to see this "thing" that invaded my body without my consent. It looked huge to me, yet they told me it was magnified on the screen. I knew that to be true, but it still looked big to me. I watched as she inserted the lanacaine needle back and forth around this thing until I was numb. Then I watched as she inserted the needle in a few different positions, hearing the "click" of the instrument clipping pieces of this tumor. I heard about 6 clips, and after that, I stopped counting

Once she was done, they tried to stop the bleeding. They inserted two clips into my breast, one for each incision in my breast for each biopsy, and told me they were there to make it easier for the surgeon...and that they were in me for life. Now I'm getting a bit concerned.

I walked into the waiting room and saw only Colleen there. I knew I had to do something to lighten the moment, so I flung open the gown I had on and said to her "look at this!" She laughed, yet we both knew it wasn't funny. Both of us said and did whatever we could to keep ourselves from feeling the seriousness of my situation. I went back in for a mammogram and they taped me up. We're done now.

I'm now wearing my old workout tank to compress the area and the bandages are sticking out from the top. Not a pretty sight and a bit scary for anyone seeing it. Colleen said we should take a picture together of this day; that I'm wearing my "badge of courage." And we did. She dropped me off home, and as the lonely night wore on, the emotions started.

I'm trying not to be angry at the people who I thought would have called to check on me, yet there were so many others who called, texted, and messaged me. The anger is not me, and I know this too shall pass.

So many emotions and so little time. I'm not enjoying this rollercoaster of feeling fine to suddenly being in tears. A few important people in my life let me down tonight, and hurt my feelings. I feel like this "journey of mine" is too much for some to handle, too much of an inconvenience in their lives. I'd like to say I'm sorry to them for that but I won't. Trust me, this is an inconvenience to my life, yet I'm handling it with grace and dignity, with humor, and with all positive thoughts. And so the journey continues...

All these feelings are not those of the usual "me", but nothing is typical of "me" at the moment. Yes, I'm going through a storm of my own right now, and at the moment, the rainbow of friends is fading more and more, day by day. I am hoping that time proves me wrong; that THEY prove me wrong.

On with the day, another lonely night, and hopefully sleep will come tonight. Yet on a positive note, I do feel the old me slipping back into place; the upbeat, positive happy girl who all these friends are counting on me to be. I'm counting on it more.

"It's More Than A Bump in the Road to My Happiness"

July 20, 2013

Once again, sleep was not so easy last night. It found me well after midnight, and took off around 5am this morning. As I lay there, thoughts, as usual, were flying through my head.

It's becoming a long weekend since the biopsy on Thursday. It's the "waiting game" now, and as positive as I've kept myself, an outburst or two emerges out of nowhere for no reason at all. Last night was a long night. I admit that under normal circumstances I talk a lot, and that comes from my love of life and people whom I meet. Now it seems I'm talking even more, at least when I have someone there to listen. I realize that I'm doing this to prevent the silence. My thoughts focus on nothing but this "thing" I'm dealing with when I'm not talking. Last night was lonely, especially since it was a Friday night and everyone I knew was out, just as they should be. On a normal day, I would have been out, too.

It was during the silence that I realized that I've been very selfish. Yes, this is MY cancer, MY thing, yet there are those in my life going through the same "waiting game" as me. I lost sight that there are those worried for me...the most important people are my children. My daughter is angry, much more than normal. My three boys just see the bandages right now when they look at their mother, and I see the look of concern in their eyes. My 12-year-old son is constantly hugging me, carefully, and making sure "he doesn't hurt me." He's telling me he loves me much more than normal, and is always asking how I feel. He's also asking a lot of questions about what may or may not happen with this "thing." My 16-year-old son has a job to keep him busy, but when he's home he just looks at me with sadness and is constantly assuring me that it's all going to be fine. My 19-year-old son stays hidden, but when he does come out of the room he seems to have barricaded himself in, he tries to act normal, yet again, all eyes see the bandages, and our conversations are much shorter than normal.

It was through my children's eyes that I realized that they're on this journey too, and they're playing the "waiting game" right along with me. It's a lot to ask of your children, and nothing I asked them to do. Yet they're my babies, and believe me to be this strong, positive mom that can fix anything. Oh, how I wish I could fix this. Until the test results of the biopsy are in, I can't fix anything. Once they're in, I'll know how to "fix" this best I can.

I'm sorry to my children and to those close to me for losing sight of your feelings, of your fears and concerns. I'm not one to be selfish, and I apologize for this. Forgive me, because it's hard to forgive myself for my selfishness.

It's the beginning of what will most likely be another long day, yet on a positive note, it's another day closer to finding out everything I need to know. My journey continues, the only difference with it today is that I know it's not just MY journey…it's "OUR" journey.

"The Unveiling"

July 20, 2013

The morning morphed into a martini glass of tears. If it had really been a martini, I would have been falling down drunk! I have no idea where the tears came from, but once they started, they wouldn't stop. Anger set in like no one's business. I want to be in my old house, sitting on my second story deck looking out over my enchanted forest and the lake. Instead, I look out over the off ramp to the highway and rather than the sound of wildlife, it's the sound of cars, trucks, and motorcycles. Good reason to be angry.

I had a hair appointment today to have more highlights. I wanted to cancel it and crazy as it sounds, all I could think of was "get it done now; it might be the last time you have hair." I poured what seemed like the fourth martini glass of tears.

None of these emotions or thoughts made sense. I never think this way. Yet the oncologist liaison at the hospital warned me of this. I thought she was kidding and that she didn't know me well enough to know that nothing gets me down, no matter what. Guess she knew better.

I went to the hairdresser anyway, and thankfully I've known them for 20 years, so the fifth martini glass of tears there didn't cause me embarrassment. I was among very dear friends. I came home with beautiful hair and went to sleep for two hours.

I woke up and took off the bandage. I looked in the mirror at the two incisions, broke down crying more than I had imagined, and knew at that moment that I was drowning in way too martini glasses of tears. My mom was over and just held me until the tears dried up. I was grateful to have any arms at that moment.

This sucks, and the waiting is awful. I know the whole story will unfold in two more days, but that doesn't make it easier. I'm alone, and as much as I'd like to have someone with me, I know I'd be terrible company. The tears are over now, and I'm feeling much stronger and more like the "me" that I know.

I realize I'm not "special" and that I'm one in a million women that have been through this, yet it doesn't make it easier. I know that I'll be fine, and as I've said before, it's the "getting from today until the fine" that worries me.

WAKING UP

I'm done with the martinis today, and have settled in with a glass of wine and my writing. I hope that these journal entries make a difference in one busy woman's life to realize that they haven't paid enough attention to their health, and that "my" journey does not have to become "their journey."

Everything happens for a reason, and if I'm going to have to go through this, it's not going to be in vain. It's going to be to make a difference in someone else's life, and maybe, just maybe, save their life. Until tomorrow, be well, be smart, and take care of yourself.

"For Today, There's Peace"

July 21, 2013

I woke up this morning feeling like my old self. No tears, no sadness, no fear, just good 'ol positive "me." Thank God! I hate to cry and yesterday threw me for a loop! I never get like that.

Today I'm saying my prayers and setting my intentions that the test results are in tomorrow. I've had enough of the waiting. Once the results are in, I can move on with what needs to be done, or what doesn't.

Call me crazy, but as much I don't like this situation, I'm learning to embrace it and love it. It came to change my life and perhaps even change me, all for the better. "If you love something, set it free…" and that's where I'm ending that old quote. I'll love the cancer, deal with it, and set it free, and no, I don't want it to come back to me.

Life hands us all sorts of wonderful blessings', and with those also comes some trials and tribulations. The key is to combine them into one, finding the blessing that you'll eventually come to find by going through the trials and tribulations.

I woke up this morning well rested, happy, and thanking God for a new day and for all the wonderful blessings I have in my life. I'm having breakfast with my cousin, Karen, a two-time breast cancer survivor, and then just letting the day take me where it will. Today I have peace and that's a blessing all by itself.

"Anxiously Awaiting"

July 23, 2013

I was disappointed the results weren't in yesterday, but at least I know I'll have the answers today. Strangely enough, I woke up with so much energy and positive thoughts! No matter what they tell me, I'm ready to hear it and move forward for what needs to be done, or doesn't.

I was grateful that a friend of mine called and took me out to dinner last night. As tired as we both were, it was great to feel like my old self. I showered, did my hair, put on make-up, and a nice dress. First time since the biopsy I felt completely like my old self, and normal. It was great to get out and be "me."

So, for today, my intention is to keep busy until the hospital calls. Cleaning, writing, building my business.... all things that should work!

I'll keep you all posted, and hopefully by tonight the next phase of "my journey" will be written and shared to many, so that "my journey" doesn't become "their journey!"

"The Waiting is Over; The Results Are In"

July 25, 2013

It was late Tuesday that the hospital called. I knew in my heart that it was cancer, and in one phone call, I knew for sure. The three or four calcium masses are all precancerous; not so bad. The tumor is an infiltrating, ductal carcinoma, grade III, 1 cm in size; not so good. It's deeper than they thought. The doctor referred me to a surgeon and told me to try to get an appointment soon. So, there I was, wondering who to call first. I haven't told that many people, but needed to let them know the results. I shed no tears at hearing the results, and assured the doctor that I was fine. I'm a positive person, and in turn they assured me that they knew this about me by simply meeting me and getting to know me during my biopsy day.

I sat my children down and told them what I knew, and that they shouldn't worry, and promised them that I would do whatever it took to kick this cancer's ass! I told them that this would not be something that would kill me. I explained that it may be a rough road, but until I saw a surgeon, we really wouldn't know the course of treatment. I joked it off as best as I could, and yet, in a strange way, I really was joking it off. It's just cancer, and I'm just the girl to knock it on its butt! Thankfully, and yet sadly, my children have been watching me fight all my life, and this was one time I was thankful for all we've gone through together in this lifetime. They know I'm strong, and know that if anyone can fight this and fix this...it's their mom.

It's quite a journey I'm embarking on, and feels so strange to simply say "I have cancer." I've become very educated over the last few days on this new terminology, and feel as though I'm learning a new language. In reality, it IS a new language, and one I wouldn't have chosen to learn.

I waited until the next day to post this to my social media page. My intention was to bring awareness to someone who may have forgotten to pay attention to their own health. I posted my "cancer" by 6 am, and by 11pm I had over 80 posts and 15 personal emails. I knew I had touched several women in realizing that they were behind in their mammograms or had just never gotten one. Success: my cancer had just touched many people, and they will never know how they touched me by their comments to me. I'm just a single mom of five children, no one special, and yet so many people I knew well, and so many I barely knew, all saw a strength in me, and found me an inspiration. Amazing, flattering, and unbelievable! I'm not that special, but with all the emotions of this cancer, they made me feel like I was here for a reason, and that having cancer wasn't going to be in vain.

This is the most surreal, yet realistic, thing I've ever gone through. I'm blessed to have so much support of so many people. As another day closes, I realize that the cancer cannot define me, and that is more of a fight than fighting off this disease. The moment I become "the girl with cancer" is the moment I lose and the cancer wins. And for anyone who knows a woman…we don't like to lose… we love to be right!

Go ahead cancer, try to define me, I dare you. It'll never happen, and I will say this with all my heart as you begin this battle to win: you will die trying!

"A Glimmer of Hope"

July 27, 2013

I met with the surgeon the other day. I loved her. She treats the mind, body and soul, and I knew just by that I had met the surgeon who would see me through this; then came the glimmer of hope. She felt that by my pathology reports and films that it presented as a Stage 1 cancer...very good! She did say that until she was actually doing the surgery she wouldn't know the exact stage. She did a breast exam and felt another lump and ordered an MRI. The lump, she believed, may be nothing more than a hematoma, a blood clot, situated close to the biopsy incision. No worries, she said, and that the MRI would tell. This "new" lump was not on the films, which is a good sign and indicative of a hematoma. Then came the best possible news...she felt a lumpectomy with radiation would be the way to treat this! No hair loss, just a few minor side effects, and that she'd monitor me like a hawk for months after. I can definitely live with this! Chemo was my worst nightmare, and this amazing woman just gave me a year of my life back that I thought I'd already lost.

I had the MRI yesterday and the result will be in within the next 48 hours. I meet with her again on Thursday. My intentions are set, my decisions made... this cancer is going to be gone, and should it reappear in time, it will be when the time is right for me, not the cancer! My younger boys need me, and losing a year of my life to chemo is robbing them of a year of their life, and anyone that knows me as a mom, knows that I will not do that to them. My belief, not hope, is that this will all go the way I want it to. There's no reason for doubt, or negativity... all good thoughts and positive intentions set.

I will say one thing about cancer, and I do know that every day you live with it, your thoughts can change. For today, I know it can be a very lonely place. Seems the people closest to you don't know quite how to deal with it, so they get angry or they stay away from you. What they don't understand is that by walking away, or treating you differently, is hurtful. I accept that not everyone knows what to do, but cancer has NOT changed me, it never will. Their reaction to my cancer changes me, because their anger and avoidance puts me in the category of "the girl with cancer." I'm just "the girl who cancer has paid a visit to" and if all goes well, it will be a short visit. I don't want to be treated like I'm sick, because I'm not. I don't want to be avoided, because I need these people to be in my life as they were just a few short days ago before the diagnosis. I don't want their pity or sympathy, I want their prayers and support, and I want their friendship as it was just days ago.

Throughout the last two weeks, I've only had two weepy days. Every other day has been the same for me. Loving my life, and all that goes with it, and never taking anything or anyone for granted. My life is not stopping because of breast cancer, my life is moving forward in spite of it.

"Taking the Day Off"

July 28, 2013

    I woke up early, and thankfully, had a reason to get in the car. I was out of coffee! So off I went, and grabbed my camera on the way out of the door. Stopped at the store for a hot cup of coffee, and the car seemed to want to steer itself straight to the beach! As a Jersey Girl, the beach has always been the place I run to when I need to run, the place I can go to think when I need to think, and the only place I can find my peace when I can't find it at home. So, 6 am, there I was, sitting on the beach in Belmar.

    If you're lucky enough to live near the ocean, then you're lucky enough. It was a beautiful morning, slightly overcast, but that didn't stop the sun from looking so beautiful. I sat there smelling the ocean and listening to the waves' crashing on the shore.

    My first thoughts were of how blessed I am that this cancer is not going to beat me, and that as the last few days have unfolded, the treatment plan isn't looking as bad as in the first few days. All the right people are lined up, from friends to professionals, to see me through this. Then, as I sat there longer, I made a decision to take the day off from any thoughts of cancer. It doesn't consume my every waking moment, not by a long shot. Should I allow that, it will have won, and there's no way I'm losing on this one. So, I let my mind shut that out and open up to thoughts of my life before this started.

    I'm blessed, I really am, and so grateful for so many things. No sadness today over those who have disappointed me a bit. They'll find their way of dealing with this, just as I have. Good things take time, and we all have to have the patience to allow each other to have that time without judgement or anger. I'm doing just that. They're in my prayers just as much as I'm sure I'm in theirs.

    So for this day, this beautiful Sunday morning, I'm taking the day off from cancer, and it's going to have to take the day off from me. Life is moving forward so beautifully, and I am grateful that I have a heart and mind that can take this journey and find all good things in it, that I can accept it for what it is, and that all good things will come from this experience.

    Enjoy your day, enjoy every day! Life can be uncertain, but the mind of a heart holds a peace that only you can bring to it. Of that I'm certain.

"Just When You Thought It Was Safe… WTF!"

July 29, 2013

The doctor called this morning with great news! The MRI results showed that the new lump they found was exactly what they thought it was: a blood clot. I began to breathe again! Then she proceeded to say that the MRI found an "enhancement" on the left breast. Breathing just got held for a minute. Here's where the "WTF" came in. Seriously? I'm out of the woods for a minute and now I'm back hiking? Here we go again. She's ordering an enhanced MRI biopsy as soon as she can.

I'm not upset over this; I still have my intentions strongly set on how this cancer is going to behave. Yet, this is another glitch, a waiting game, a test of my patience which can be less of a virtue for me these days. I know that it's part of the process, and truth be told, I am much luckier than some at how quickly I have gotten appointments and results. I've gotta believe that this biopsy will be the same. The doctor doesn't think she can do it until next week, yet I've been doing pretty good so far at "willing" what I want, so I'm willing a Thursday or Friday biopsy. Praying to the Guy upstairs to help, too!

I'm not thrilled at going back in the "tank" again. MRI's of any kind are simply not my cup of tea. Yet, I'll do it with a little help from a mild sedative and a headset playing some kick ass music!

The call this morning did stop me in my tracks, and the plans I made for today are on hold, but just for today. I've had a million calls to make for scheduling this test and that test. I feel the need to do some mindless cleaning to get my mind off it all, then do all my paperwork and writing. Sometimes all the things that come with cancer are exhausting, and I'm feeling tired already.

For today, I clean, I dance, I write, I sing, I laugh, I do stupid paperwork. And for tomorrow? I dance, I write, I sing, I laugh…and get back out with my business and on with my life!

"Those Who Matter Don't Mind"

July 30, 2013

This week seems to be practically over even though it's only Tuesday. I have an appointment tomorrow, the surgeon on Thursday and reiki on Friday. On Saturday I leave for a three-hour drive to see my godson married. Home on Sunday. Perhaps this is why I'm feeling so tired. My entire sleep schedule is out of whack, along with my breast! Maybe it's all this "positive, adrenaline pumping energy" I have that's making me tired.

I know part of it is a phone call last night that I was dreading and wishing would not go in the direction that it did. Actually, in my heart, I already knew where it was going to go, and no amount of wishing or praying it wouldn't, didn't stop it from going where it did. This fatigue may be the result of every day he's been distancing himself from me more and more. Cancer isn't making me tired, the loss of a dear friend is. Sleep turns the world off for awhile, while being awake makes you feel it. I don't like feeling it.

Cancer hasn't made me feel sad; it's actually made me stronger. His reaction to it made me sad, and backing away from me made me feel weak. I understand everyone handles things differently and reacts differently. My question is this: "who walks away from a friend because they don't want to handle or hear about their cancer?" My answer: "no friend of mine."

Here's where I change. I felt hurt and angry. Today, his actions lit a fire inside of me to move forward without him. I'll mourn the loss of a friend I loved, and that's where it ends. Cancer hasn't hurt as much as his selfish actions, yet I know he will soon be learning new lessons in his life from my cancer. We all learn lessons in life, and my cancer is a lesson for me, for anyone who knows me, and for those who know me by my writing. In the end the lessons make us grow, teach us what they came to teach us, and make our life better. His life will change, too, and I hope for the better. One of my favorite lines from the book "Eat, Pray, Love" by Elizabeth Gilbert, is "miss him, wish him light and love, and drop it." I will miss him (I already do), I will wish him well (I already am), and I will drop it (I already have).

What I know for sure today is that I really am much "braver, stronger, and smarter" than I thought.

"This Is The Time of My Life"

July 31, 2013

Finally, a day without feeling exhausted. So, here I am: hair done, make-up on, wearing my favorite "island" dress and ready to head out for the day. A few clients this morning and then an afternoon of pampering for me. A much-needed afternoon!

Cancer is a funny thing. When there's a lull in doctor appointments and hospital visits, I actually forget I even have it. I know that time will be coming to an end soon, especially since I have to see the surgeon tomorrow for more results of the tests. Yet the last few days, despite all that's been going on, I've realized more than ever is that I'm simply the same old girl who just happens to have a lump in her breast that has cancer.

I'm working on a huge project for Breast Cancer Awareness that will not only help so many women, but also another business so near and dear to my heart. I can't say what that is yet, but I'll let you know when it's all set up and ready to go. Throughout this morning, I realized more than ever that the cancer came for many reasons, and that this is truly "the time of my life." A time of changes and even more so, a time to make a difference in so many lives, and just maybe, a difference in the world. Now, that's a gift, and one that I'm grateful for: one lump in my breast and a million ways to make a difference from it.

My wish for everyone is to take everything that comes into your life, good or bad, and find an opportunity in it to help someone else. It doesn't matter who you are, where you are, or what you are, everyone counts, and everyone can choose to make a difference in someone's life. It makes the "journey" so much more worth it.

"It's All In Your Perspective"

August 5, 2013

I haven't written in a few days, mostly because last Thursday was the day of the final results of my tests with the surgeon, and my emotions were flying. I also had a very special weekend in Hershey, PA, to watch my godson get married. He just happens to be my best friend, Colleen's, son!

First things first: I went to the surgeon on Thursday, and I will forever be grateful to Colleen's mom for being there with me. She's a retired oncology nurse, and was more than helpful at asking the surgeon questions that I wouldn't know to ask. I sat there as the surgeon pulled out my chart and said, "I'm so sorry, but we have to do a mastectomy of the right breast, and because of the cancerous cells on the left side, it's best to do a double mastectomy." Ok, I was ready for that news. I wasn't ready for what came next. "No, I'm sorry, but everything has to be removed from your breast, no nipple sparing." The best news of all of this was that I would not have to have chemo or radiation. Call that my biggest blessing of my breast cancer! Ok, tears started falling. She handed me a tissue and proceeded to tell me about all the necessary steps I'd have to take in my home, my children's lives, and more importantly, in my life. A plastic surgeon was already in place for me to do the reconstruction during the surgery, and I meet with him on Wednesday. She'd like to do the surgery within the next two to three weeks.

The surgeon told me to prepare for all of this now, as even without chemo or radiation, the recovery is long and painful. So, she said: "Whatever things you need to do now, get them done. Prepare your house for your recovery, move things to arm level because you will not be able to raise your arms. Make your bedroom a room of comfort and easy access, because you will be in bed quite often, and if there's anything you want to do, go do it. Get out with friends and have fun." I don't have a surgery date yet, but once I have it, the countdown begins.

She left the office, and I just put my head in my hands and sobbed. Colleen's mom held me for what seemed like forever. Her voice was comforting and compassionate, and I was thankful that this was one appointment I brought someone with me, because other than my biopsy with Colleen, I have done this all alone. Her mom gave me a lot of great advice to prepare for this and took me home.

I couldn't hide the sobbing from my kids, so explained it all to them as I cried. I told them I wasn't crying because I was scared, because I wasn't. "I'm not going

WAKING UP

to die, and I'm not going to be sick from chemo," I told them. "I'm crying because I'm very sad at losing something so important to me as a woman, something that defines a woman as a woman." They looked scared, and it broke my heart to see their faces. This was "our" reality now and it's coming soon. We'll do this together with grace and dignity, just as we have through every other trial and tribulation we've faced together as a family.

I spent the entire day and night sobbing, and knew that I needed to get it all out. I woke up the next day with a new perspective: out with the old, in with the new. Cancer was not getting my life, just taking my breasts. Cancer was not robbing me of a year or more of my life with chemo, it was just taking a few months of recovery. Cancer was not winning this; I was and I am. I'll have beautiful new "tatas" by next spring, and while they won't be the same as the original set, they'll be better! They will be my reward at that end of this battle, and I will wear them as a beautiful badge of courage that I fought and won!

I haven't shed another tear since last Thursday, yet I'm sure as my surgery date is set and get's closer, tears may fall here and there. And that's alright. I've had such amazing support from people I barely know, and mere acquaintances are becoming very dear friends. I've also felt the hurt in my heart of good friends and family walking away from me. Cancer doesn't just affect the body, but it affects those around you, and not always in the way you'd expect.

All things happen for a reason, and I have the choice to change what I can. So, I'm changing my perspective. Take my breasts, cancer, go ahead. You already decided on that, but you are not taking my life, or my will, or my positive outlook.

Having cancer is like stepping into a boxing ring for the biggest fight of the century. For me, the bell has run, and I'm the one that the announcer is saying "And the winner is…" yet I already know who won…ME!

"Save The Date"

August 11, 2013

I was at the shop on Thursday afternoon picking up my car when I received a call from the doctor's office. They asked if I was going to be home soon. I told them I hadn't planned on it, and they proceeded to tell me the breast surgeon needed to speak with me so I should go home. That couldn't be good, so I left the shop and headed home. Another way of cancer screwing up my plans for the day.

It was at 4pm when my doctor called. First off, my surgery date is August 21st. As I write this now, that's just 10 days to get my house cleaned and sterile, get my kids life and my own in order. The pressure was certainly building. What she said next was something I was completely unprepared for. She told me that my case was presented before "the board" and I knew that meant that my case was not standard Breast Cancer 101. Sure wasn't. I tested positive for HER2NU, which is not good. Not good at all. It's basically a protein that attaches itself to cancer cells, and promotes the spreading of the cancer throughout your body. Gee, wasn't ready for that. What came next I was most definitely NOT ready to hear… or do! Her feeling and that of the boards was to do the surgery, followed by a triple chemo cocktail for 3-6 months and a year of a drug called "Herceptin," which is a cutting edge cancer drug that literally encapsulates this HER2NU protein. Guess you could say it's the latest "life saving" drug.

My first response to my wonderful doctor was "stick it up your ass, I'm not doing chemo." No way. I'm getting pissed now. "First you want my breasts, now my hair, what next? Me? I'm not doing." In her soft-spoken fashion, she said "I'm glad you're angry. That's healthy. You're attitude is wonderful but you need to feel these feelings at times. You need chemo or you will die." At that moment I didn't care. Not one bit. I ranted at her for a bit, and she graciously, and lovingly, allowed it. She apologized for the news, but my case is different, and dangerous.

I pulled out a bottle of wine, and began sobbing from a place so deep inside of me that I never knew it existed. I called Colleen, and I could swear I heard her crying too. She researched this for me, and agreed with the doctor. I'm becoming a ticking time bomb, and throughout all Colleen's research, the treatment was the same: chemo! I'm screwed now, and life just changed even more.

That night was the only time, and the last time, I ever asked "why me?" I have never questioned why anything in my life has happened, but I did now. I just

WAKING UP

lost that year and half of my life as I knew it; that year and a half I thought I had gotten back. I felt such anger and fear…two emotions that are so foreign to me, that I just didn't know what to do with them. I'm always looking at the bright side, and keeping positive, but at 4pm on Thursday that all went out the window, and I turned into someone I never knew. Thank God for wine, a few close friends that let me sit on the phone and sob and yell and bitch like I never have in my life. Sleep came by 1am, and I'm sure that happened because I had simply worn myself out.

I woke up on Friday with the same emotions, and completely exhausted. I took a nap, and I woke up as my old self. It was nothing short of a miracle. Since Friday afternoon, I have decided to live, no matter what it would take to do. Cancer and chemo are, I'm sure, on some days to come, going to knock me flat on my face and kick my ass. Go ahead because cancer screwed with the wrong girl when it picked me, and as hard as it may kick my ass, I intend to and promise to kick its ass back so hard it won't know what hit it!

My biggest fear, outside of losing my breasts, my hair, my life, was of losing "myself." I wondered if cancer could and would do that, too, leaving nothing but a shell of my old self. I've decided it won't, it can't, and there is no way I will let it.

Today I am cleaning my house and arranging it in a "recovery feng shui" sort of look. Cancer has taken control of many things in my life, but my recovery is MY way of controlling what I can. I want my recovery to be one of grace and dignity, a lot of ass kicking, and all the while doing it in a home that is peaceful and pretty.

This cancer crap sucks, and is such an inconvenience in my life. Yet, I still believe there's a reason, and I will keep an open mind and heart while waiting for that reason to come.

Watch out, cancer, I'm watching you every step of the way. And trust me, I have a lot of people supporting and praying for me. You don't have a chance in hell of surviving, so enjoy your time with me while you can. I promise you…it won't last long!

"When Your Breasts' Do The Talking!"

August 13, 2013

I have eight more nights with this set of breasts, and boy, are they talking! Funny what you start thinking about as the clock is ticking. Let's see, I want to finish getting my house ready, I want to go on a motorcycle ride, I want at least two nights out of dinner and drinks with friends, what I consider my "Bye Bye Boobie" party, I want one more afternoon at Wall Stadium with my drivers and I want to make love one more time while my breasts are still here.

Yes, well, best laid plans don't always happen. I'm hoping to be able to fulfill at least two of the above. My guess is it will be dinner with the girls and Wall Stadium with the guys. Every day now is filled with cancer stuff that needs to be handled. I thought the week before "the girls" leave my body for good that I would at least have a week of calm and doing what I want. It's been anything but that. I'm emotionally drained from talking about it and dealing with it all day, that by 7pm, when I'd be getting ready to go out for fun, I'm too tired to do it.

I have handled this all with a positive attitude since Day 1, and I'm still handling it well. I trust all the professionals I'm dealing with, and have complete confidence in them. Yet, there are certain people who are hell-bent on disrupting this for me, and that's one more thing added to all this that I don't need and don't want. Cancer gave me a voice, that's for sure, but there are those I have no voice for, and when I have, they don't hear me.

If I can hear my breasts talking, surely these people can hear me. I know they feel out of control, yet it's not their cancer or body to control, it's mine. And no matter how much I explain this, they've blocked it all. I know that they are scared for me, and feel helpless, but taking away my control of this is not a good thing. They are entitled to their feelings, and I wouldn't judge them for it, but over stepping their bounds and going over my head is something I cannot tolerate. I'm sure you can hear the resentment through my words. And my feelings of that are okay too, but I would rather not have them to feel it at all.

Enough with complaining and on with doing what my breasts want, and that is finding some "me" time before next week. I've decided that Friday will be my day of no phone for a few hours and some relaxation. One more trip to the hairdresser to get my roots touched up. After all, I won't be starting chemo for a few weeks after the surgery, so until then, I'm keeping my hair just as it is. Should

I lose it when chemo start's, at least I lose it with no gray roots! After that, I think a manicure and pedicure are in order. It's my day and I intend to have it.

One of my best friends, Theo, called last night with such a great surprise: he's flying up from Florida on Saturday morning, and leaving late Sunday. He's sorry it's only one night, but that gesture meant the world to me! So, I guess I will have a night of dinner and drinks, and will introduce him to my drivers at the track and my Angel girlfriends. I want them to all join together through social media and phone numbers to keep a positive chain of love and support wrapped tightly around me, and they are just the people to do it.

I'm blessed to be a writer. Even as I write this, I can feel the stress dwindling away, and it's a good thing. Feelings are expressed through my writing, and it seems to wash the negative ones away. It's as good as talking to a good friend.

And at this moment, I am blessed and grateful for so many good friends, and even more so for all the new ones dropping into my life. Angels? Yes, I believe in spiritual angels, and I also believe in all these "Earth Angels" in my life. Doesn't get any better than that!

"Second Opinions Lead to Different Decisions"

August 17, 2013

My family decided to step in quite forcefully and make me get a second opinion. Let me tell you, I literally went kicking and screaming last Thursday to a cancer institute that they made an appointment at. They knew I was angry about it, and I was going to cancel the appointment without even telling them, but I didn't. I knew if I did that I'd never hear the end of it, and that it would cause a lot of problems in our relationship and knowing that I'd need their help with my recovery, it wasn't the smartest thing for me to do. So, I decided I'd go, against my will, and waste a precious day of doing other things I wanted to do before my surgery.

My dad picked me up at 11am, and I ranted for the first ten minutes of the drive, to which he said "Are you done yet? I thought we could make this a fun adventure!" Only my dad! I looked at him and said "Yes, I'm done, but I'm not happy about any of this." He said he knew, and my dad, who is a laid back, easy-going guy looked at me and explained that no matter how old I was, I was still his child, and that his child had cancer, and they are all scared. He explained that they all handle it differently, and that while he's handling it pretty well, my mom isn't. While I appreciated his honesty, I felt terrible. The hospital was about an hour away, and we got there a little before 1pm. My sister-in-law met us there. My dad opted to stay in the waiting room, while she went in with me.

My second opinion went on with a breast surgeon and oncologist for over four hours, which I'll admit, was much more time than my original surgeon had spent with me, and I had never even seen an oncologist with her. I hate to admit that I'm wrong, but I was. This was much more education than I had gotten to so far, and I began feeling grateful to my family for pushing the second opinion on me.

The surgeon told me that he feels I've had this cancer for five years, 250 weeks! Wow, I was shocked! He also felt that chemo for 6 months first, then see what type of surgery was necessary, was the best way to go, and the way they have had more success with. Kill the cancer first, especially not knowing if it's spread or not, then worry about the surgery. Made sense to me.

The oncologist was amazing. Same chemo cocktail as my original surgeon, but agreeing to hit the cancer cells head on first, and do more biopsies and a cat scan all throughout the chemo. She also measured my tumor, which was 1 cm. in size back in July, and is now 2.5 cm. It sure is a fast-moving, aggressive tumor. At this point, they want to shrink it fast.

Basically, this was the same procedures my original surgeon had suggested, just in a different order. I had so much to think about, yet I was beginning to see their treatment plan as making much more sense. After six months of chemo, they said it may turn out to be just a lumpectomy, but at least if it wasn't, I'd be prepared for a mastectomy. Also, instead of my doctors plan of mastectomy, chemo, reconstruction, which was a lot of surgeries, these doctors felt that could do mastectomy and reconstruction all at once, if in fact I needed the mastectomy.

So, I thought about it all night, and after 2 glasses of wine, called my brother and thanked him for making me go. He knows that their way of doing this was not the best, but they just wanted me to do this for myself and my children. I was glad they did.

I called my surgeon on Friday morning, and asked many more questions. She wasn't happy about my having the second opinion, took me off the surgery schedule, and told me I was making a huge mistake and would regret it. I was shocked at her reaction, and thought it very unprofessional. And to be honest, that was what made my mind up 100% to go with the cancer institute. Even if I was to choose my surgeon, that shipped sailed with her attitude. There would be no way I'd let someone who talked to me that way perform any surgery on me.

In the end, by Friday afternoon, I picked Door #2, and I prayed to God that I picked the right one. It's funny that when your life is on the line and the decisions of treatment to save your life in your hands, you go by your gut. I closed my eyes, said a prayer to God to give me the right answer, and in my head, and my heart, I heard "second opinion." Most of those I know support my decision, and my family is relieved and so happy that I will be treated at a cancer institute. I know I am too. Yet, I will admit, I hope this was the right choice.

Chemo starts in less than two weeks, and a new journey of my cancer begins. I should be done with chemo in March, my birthday month, and nothing would make me happier to know I had kicked chemo's ass by my birthday!

For today, I'm picking up my friend, Theo, at the airport, for his one night visit, and on Wednesday my girlfriend is flying up for 5 days! I know the things I want to do before chemo starts, and have called the appropriate friends to do them for me…and yes, looks like I'll be getting my motorcycle ride after all! I want to have "the time of my life" before this journey begins.

I called the cancer institute yesterday afternoon and told them to sign me up, and they certainly did. I hung up the phone, and for the first time in days I took a breath, let it go, and put it all in God's hands.

"Oh, The Things You Will Think When You Have Cancer!"

August 19, 2013

There's a lot of thoughts that run through your mind when you have cancer, and with chemo looming in about 10 days, there is so much more to think about. Fortunately, I'm keeping my sense of humor about it, at least for the time being, and find myself laughing with my friends about the silliest of "thinks I am thinking!"

1. I wear my glasses on top of my head all the time, because if I misplace them, I can't see a thing when I read. My girlfriend, Terilyn, was over the other morning, a bit teary eyed over my cancer stuff, when I said to her: "You know, I always wear my glasses on my head. What happens when you lose your hair from chemo? Won't they just keep sliding off?" Well, she began laughing and said, "We'll get some pink velcro for the top of your head to hold them in place!"

2. I said a "good-bye" to all my drivers at Wall Stadium on Saturday, telling them that I probably wouldn't see them again until next season. Colleen thought I was saying "good-bye" because I'm dying…not true. She said you can still go there even with chemo or if you lose your hair. I said: "I'll have no eyelashes, and that is the dustiest place in the world, especially when they're racing. I'll get so much dust in my eyes that I'll be blind on top of it all!"

3. One of my girlfriends is coming up to visit soon, and has told me that she wants to try to do that at least once a month out to help me and the kids out if we need it. She's offered to shave my legs for me, just so I feel more "human." I chuckled at her and said, "Sweetie, if I lose the hair on my head, there will be no hair anywhere!" She laughed and said, "Well, that could be a good thing. Less maintenance!"

4. Wigs, scarves, turbans…all these crazy things to have if you should you lose your hair. I'll entertain the wig idea, but the scarves and turbans? I don't see it. Terilyn doesn't see it either, she sees me as more a "bad ass bandana" kind of girl! I see it too, so it'll be off to the Harley store this week for some bandana's and a Harley baseball hat. If I'm going to lose my hair, I'm not losing me, and truth be told, deep inside, I am a "biker chick!"

ANNE DENNISH

It's funny how you can turn a somber mood of thinking of all the "not so good things" that will happen with chemo into something to laugh about. This is one trait about myself that I'm glad I have.

Nowadays when I want my kids to do something, and they're not doing it, my son will tell me I'm about to play the "C" card! To which I reply, "Life handed me the deck, and I'm playing the card!" I'm finding that the more I joke about it (and we all know that this is serious) the more they do, too. I'm praying that we can keep this up all throughout this journey we're about to embark on. Laughter is the best medicine, and I'm glad my babies are with me on this. I'll hear my youngest laughing with his friends on-line and hear him going, "But my mom has cancer! She can't bake you brownies!" So glad he can do that, because while I can bake brownies, I don't feel like doing it!

I pray that my family can maintain a sense of humor through this, because I am sure there will be days that none of us feel like laughing. They've seen me have a few emotional days, and thankfully, not very many, yet the one thing I don't allow them to see is my fear, because believe me, I'm scared. I'll hide the fear from them, because the moment they see it in me, I'll see it even more in them, and I don't want that.

I asked my friend for two things before he leaves next week…a ride on his Harley, and two dresses from the island. He was surprised that's all I asked for, especially since I have never asked him for anything. I thought about it for a moment and told him I'd email him a new list! Now is not the time to be the "low maintenance" kind of girl I usually am. I'm shooting for the moon this week, and if that list was too short, he'll be surprised when he gets his email this morning. And I know he'll laugh when he gets it.

Dr. Seuss always has words of wisdom, and "Oh the thinks you can think" is one of my favorites, because the truth is, when you have cancer you think a million different thoughts, most of mine positive, yet some not so positive. So I will continue to "think the thinks I can think" and look forward to my next Dr. Seuss moment: "Oh the places you'll go!" I'm off and running to kick the ass of this cancer, and when it's all said and done, I'll be off to a new beginning in my life of a million different "places I can go!"

"My Point of Impact"

August 22, 2013

I had a great night on Tuesday, and an even better morning on Wednesday. I went up to the hospital for tests, only to find out I couldn't have it done. So, off I went to my old job to use the fax machine. What happened to me there changed my thinking and my perspective, and perhaps, in the long run, my strength into not letting this cancer take away my life for the next year. It was one of the most important "points of impact" I've had since learning I had cancer. Let me begin at the beginning...

I started writing for Wall Stadium Speedway last summer, interviewing the drivers in my own column. Most people didn't know I wasn't paid to do this, and those that did thought I was crazy to work for free. For me, it was a chance to be a journalist, not just a writer, and to get my name out there. I also knew that every time I walked through the gates of the pits that something wonderful was coming into my life from it, and it did, so many more ways than I would have ever imagined.

I met so many drivers that first season who have become some of my biggest supporters with all that I am going through and have become very dear friends. Mike Tillett, aka, the Rooster, his family and I, became very close. Mike asked me to write an article a year ago about his sister, Patty, who has cancer. She became my best friend after meeting, yet it's funny how a year later I would be writing about myself. On another occasion, one of the guys at the track, instant messaged me one day and asked if I would want to be a receptionist for a friend of his who owns a body shop. I told him I would and the rest is history.

I met with his friend and started working there two days later. He and I hit it off the first day, and have become very close friends. I've gotten to know his two children very well, and "love them like my own" and met some really nice friends of his. To say we're like a family is an understatement.

I loved everyone who worked there, and on a bad day at the shop, I was able to go sliding into a bay doing a crazy dance or simply smile and laugh at them to change the mood. I loved getting to know the vendors, the customers, the insurance adjusters…there wasn't a thing I didn't love about it. I left there in March to begin my own business, but still would work when the shop needed me. I've been in and out of the shop working for the last several months that one of the vendors nicknamed me the "boomerang" because I kept leaving and coming back.

Well, today changed a lot for me. Sometimes it's not the big things that change our way of thinking, but it's the simplest of things. And that's what happened yesterday…a point of impact. I stopped by the shop to use the fax machine, and ended up staying for a few hours just to help out. I realized then how very much I love that job, and how much I've missed it. And then I thought…why would I not work there if they needed me just because of cancer and chemo? Why let chemo dictate my life, when in fact, I can.

It took less than two hours at that shop for me to say "screw it… cancer sucks enough, chemo bites, but damn, I'm not letting it change my entire life!" I can't imagine that every day will be bad through chemo, and maybe that was my problem, I WAS imaging that. No more…I know life is going to change, my appearance will change, my energy may change, but I'm not letting this crap change me! I'm assuming how everyone will see me and I have to apologize to them for that, because those that mean the most to me would never see me as anything other than who I am inside. The outside may change for a while, but the inside will not, except to get more driven, stronger and ready to kick ass more than ever! As I write this I think how silly I've been in believing some crazy thoughts in my head, yet I know that that's normal when you're dealing with all this.

Well, I'm done! On with better days, smarter thinking, and a new-found "drive" that no cancer, chemo, or person will change.

Thank you Wall Stadium for allowing me to write, for all the friends you allowed me to meet, for the friends that found a job for me that I love, and thank you to my old job, for reminding me that cancer is not a reason to give up, and that my life before my cancer was still at that shop for two hours yesterday. Being there reminded me that life goes on no matter what, and that I can make that choice to keep going on with my life as I want it, no matter cancer, chemo, or anything else. Cancer may have come for a brief visit, yet it won't be here for the rest of my life…but I will!

"The Pro's and Con's of Cancer!"

August 23, 2013

My girlfriend, Colleen, and I share a lot of laughs over my cancer. It's one of the ways we cope, and for me, I've used faith and laughter to get through everything in my life. So, she suggested I write a list of the pros and cons of cancer, so here goes...

The Cons:

You have cancer

The chemo: nauseau, hair loss, feeling like you have the flu, and all those other nasty side effects

The inconvenience in your life dealing with doctors, oncologists, hospitals, support groups...all that stuff.

Dealing with family members and friends that make your cancer their drama, especially when I don't see it as a drama, just another journey in life.

Trying to be a mom to my kids when I know it's anyone's guess how chemo will affect me

The fear of the unknown.

The Pro's:

You won't have to cook because people are willing to do it for you.

You don't have to car pool, because everyone offers to do it for you.

You don't have to clean your house or do your laundry because people will offer to do it for you.

People volunteer to pick up any food you're craving and drop it off.

ANNE DENNISH

Should I lose my hair, all I have to do is wake up and throw on a wig. No blow drying involved! Also, no more Brazilian waxes or shaving my legs…very little maintenance with hair loss.

Being on steroids with chemo will naturally fill in the wrinkles on my face!

That's the short list for now. I'm trying to find laughter through all of this the best I can, and most days it works! I intend to laugh so hard at this cancer that it will have had enough of me and want to just leave…one of those "we picked the wrong girl, time to move on" moments

The long list is the time you spend kicking its' ass, but my intention is to live for another 30 or 40 years, so the time kicking cancer is nothing compared to the years of life ahead of me I intend to, and will have.

The con is having cancer in the first place…the pro is living through it and becoming a survivor. No matter what cancer hands me throughout this journey, I won't back down! I already AM a survivor!

"My Mountain is Waiting...Tomorrow's the Day"

August 28, 2013

Tomorrow is the day I face "my mountain," the chemo mountain. It's the day I put on my hiking boots, and start my journey up the mountain for the next six months. Just like any hike up a mountain you've never climbed, you feel nervous, not knowing if it will go smoothly or you will find yourself on treacherous ground. That's how I feel right now. It's going to be a difficult climb at times, I'm sure, but once I reach the top, I'll stand there proud and happy, filled with peace, knowing that at that moment I'll begin my journey down the other side of this mountain: "cancer-free." And I know that once I reach the bottom, a new, exciting life will be waiting for me, even better than the life I have now!

It's the last day my body will be this way, will look this way, or feel this way. Tomorrow at 7am I will be having surgery for a port, followed by my first round of chemo. I know that my looks won't change overnight, but they will change for awhile. As healthy as I feel at this very moment, that too will change in the next 48 hours. Life as I have known it will all change by tomorrow, and honestly, it's been changing little by little since I was diagnosed with cancer.

I've still maintained a positive attitude, an upbeat sense of humor about it all, and find myself getting stronger and stronger everyday to fight this, yet as I sit here today, knowing what's coming tomorrow, I feel anxious, feverish, nervous...and not ready for the unknown. I'm a "need to know" kind of girl, and not knowing how chemo will affect this body does make me nervous. What I do know is that I have cancer, that I will fight it, that I will not die from it, and that I will win this battle. What I don't know is the affects of toxins pulsing through my body for the next six months.

The last week has been amazing, filled with an overwhelming outpouring of love and support from so many people who I know. It's been one of having a dream come true this past weekend. For once in my life, I am so overwhelmed with feelings over the last few days that I cannot even write about it yet. The words to describe the wonder and excitement of it all escape me at this moment, but stay posted, you will see this story soon.

The clock seems to be ticking faster today, when I wish time would just stand still. I feel like I'm saying "good-bye" to the old me, and beginning a journey to see who the "new" me will be. I'm not afraid of the journey I'm about to embark on, not afraid at all. My cancer is here for a brief stay, and is here for a reason. I'm sure I will learn many lessons on this journey and I hope others do, too.

I wish there were words to thank all the wonderful friends supporting me, loving me, and being there for me throughout this. They are the "army" behind me, and they'll never know how much they all mean to me, and that their spirit is a driving force which keeps me so strong. I love them all, and will be holding them all in my heart tomorrow as I begin this journey, this "hike up my mountain."

I'll keep you all posted as best as I can, and I intend to hold up a sign tomorrow as they "beam me up" with chemo. It will say this: "Bring it on, cancer! You are about to have your ass kicked!"

"And The Climb Has Begun..."

August 30, 2013

I had to wake up at 5am yesterday, but truth be told, I never really slept. I woke up with the worst migraine headache I've ever had...no surprise. My dad picked me up at 5:30 to head to the hospital. I laid down the front seat to sleep, ice packs under my neck for the headache. By the time we got there, my migraine was in full force.

We checked in, I got ready, and soon was lined up for the port surgery. As I go along on this journey it's sad to see how prevalent cancer is. It's everywhere, and unless you're personally touched by it you don't realize just how many people are affected by it. I was first in the line-up of three, all of us waiting to have a foreign object placed into our body, so that all three of us could begin chemo.

My surgeon was funny, and began the twilight sleep. He said should I wake up and need more medicine, let him know! Seriously, who wants to wake up during that? Well, I'll admit, my snoring woke me up, at which the doctor automatically told the anesthesiologist to give me more. I felt nothing, until I woke up after it. I had, and still do, have a lot of pain in my neck, and chest where the surgery was done. I'm bruised pretty bad, and I know that will get worse over the next few days.

My dad and I actually walked from the hospital after the surgery down to the cancer institute. I had him stay close, just in case I took a tumble. I didn't want anyone to see me fall if I did. Rule of thumb for women who fall: don't let anyone see you, then check to see if you're ok!

I had a room and a nurse waiting for me, and was lucky to get some migraine medication to knock out the headache, which with sleep, it did. They hooked me up and off I went. The surreal part was that the actual chemotherapy comes in two huge syringes which the nurse has to sit and inject into your line. Pretty interesting!

It was a long day, and I didn't get home until after dinner. My kids were almost afraid to touch me, but you know me, I walked in and was like: "well, that was cool! Look at my port!" Once they knew I was okay and still the "same old mom, cracking jokes and acting silly," the house seemed peaceful without all the anxiety that's been in it for weeks now. I was up and about with them for a few hours until they crashed and I took my meds and crashed myself.

Today, after a wonderful drug induced sleep, I've gotten back onto social media and writing. I've felt great all day, still sore from the surgery, and now I notice my cheeks are flushed as if I have a fever. All normal. I'd like to believe that this is how every treatment will be, but I know better. It will get worse at I get more chemo treatments, but for today, I'm still me, still feeling good, chatting on the phone, writing, messing around with my kids…the usual!

I feel overwhelmed at the love and support from so many people. I know in my heart how blessed I am, and am incredibly grateful. I appreciate the comments on social media I get. They keep me strong!

Today is a good day, and life is good. I intend to say that everyday throughout this journey, no matter how bad it should get. Every day I wake up and see my children and hear from my friends is a "good day!"

"Life Still Goes On"

August 31, 2013

Two days after the port and the chemo, I'm feeling fine. The port still hurts a lot and the bruising is getting darker, yet I still feel pretty good. The anti-nausea medication I take twice a day does make me a bit dizzy, but for those who know me, I always am a little dizzy! In a good way!

It's kind of funny.... you feel like yourself, yet they give you all these instructions on being careful with germs, not cutting yourself in case of infection, the list goes on and on, yet I feel normal. I feel like washing the dishes, doing some laundry, even cooking, and then you think "are you supposed to?" I know I feel good; this was only the first shot of chemo, and I know when I get the next round in three weeks it may change. I'll tell you, though, I'm going to believe that this is the way my chemo will go. I'm not fooling myself into thinking I may feel worse as time goes on, but I'm not buying it right now. I feel positive and hopeful, and I just may be one of the few that get through this with minimal physical side effects. And that's what I choose to believe.

I know, the hair loss may come in time. Fine, I've accepted that. I will not accept that I will be bed ridden sick. I will not accept that I will not work again, or have a night out with friends. I will not lock myself in a germ free bubble, when in fact, my greatest risk of cold or flu will soon be walking in my front door after 3pm when they get off the public school bus! So forget the "bubble style of living" for me. I'm living careful, but not in the bubble. Life is too short, and cancer may be part of it for now, but it won't be for long.

It's been a quiet day of relaxing and sitting outside in the sun and fresh air, and hanging out watching movies with the kids. Tonite, I'm sitting outside looking at the stars and listening to the sounds of Wall Stadium. I was hoping to make it there tonight for a little while, but fatigue is upon me, and in reality, it's only been two days since the surgery and it probably would be smarter to wait until next week to go.

It's been a good day since the "climb up the mountain" began, and I am grateful for every day, good or bad. So far, good is taking precedence over bad.

As I wind the day down and get ready for sleep, I think of all the wonderful friends I have supporting me through this. I think of all the blessings in my life, and how grateful I am for all of them. I end this day with this thought: Cancer is not my life, it's just a visitor in it, and the truth is that my life is good!

"You Can Always Change, No Matter Your Age"

September 5, 2013

As we all get older, I hear so many people say "I'm too old to change." I don't believe this and never have, because I know how much I have changed over the years, and especially over the last several weeks. I knew there would be lessons from having cancer, and oh my goodness, I've had quite a few so far.

I try never to let fear enter my thoughts, and while it's perfectly fine that it does at times, I've learned how to feel it for a brief moment, then sit silently and do what it takes to release it. I kiss it up to God and fall deep into my faith. I let faith replace my fear, and to be honest, it's not always that easy, but it can be done. The more you believe this, the easier it is to actually do it. I used to live a good part of my life in fear of so many things…of dying too early and leaving young children without a mom, of financial situations that have come up, of something terrible happening to my kids. Yet, as I've gotten older, my belief is that "my life was written when I was born" and there is nothing I can do to change that. So, why not enjoy every moment, good or bad, in life, learn your lessons from each experience, and forget the fear? I changed. I changed my thinking, and the way I look at things. I've let faith rule my life, and I haven't regretted it yet, and it's worked every time. And life is much more exciting and happy without the fear!

There have been a few people who I can say made me feel bad, upset, or hurt, yet this is another way I changed. I don't judge anyone on their behavior, and don't blame anyone for making me feel badly. I allow them to make me feel badly, because truth be told, they are who they are, just as I am who I am. I will forever find the good in everyone, and believe with all my heart that there IS good in everyone. Some choose to let you see the good, others choose to hide what's in their heart. That's a choice they make, not me. I have learned to accept everyone in my life, everyone that I meet, as the person they are. No one is perfect, especially me, and I will not judge someone on who they are. This was and is another lesson, and one that I'm happy to be working on every day. We meet every person for a reason, and while some are meant to be simply a catalyst to take us to another chapter in our life, others are meant to stay briefly, while some are meant to stay a lifetime. No one can hurt you if you don't allow it. This is one of my best lessons so far: that I'm learning that I have the ability to control my feelings.

I've found my voice and my truth, throughout this. I always loved the quote "say what you mean, mean what you say, and don't be mean when you say it."

WAKING UP

When my cancer hit, I knew exactly how I wanted my treatment and recovery to be: peaceful, calm, and positive. My voice has learned to say to those in my life that cannot respect my wishes for this, and do nothing but bring negativity into my life, that I cannot have them around for now. My voice has made it clear to them that it is my choice to do this my way, and I will not settle for less.

I've learned to see my life as I want it: cancer free, healthy, successful, and happy. To me, at this moment, I am all of those. The next few months are simply part of the journey to get me there, yet I live each day as though "I already am there." I've always known how positive I am in life, yet over the last two months, I've impressed myself at how much more positive I am, and more so, how strong my will is. There are days I wonder if I'm just talking myself into these feelings, yet I know that would take way too much energy, and I'd end up being exhausted all the time. I'm none of these, and I know in my heart and down to my toes, I am positive, I am sure, and I do have a will stronger than the cancer.

I'm a loving person, and cancer has strengthened that so much more. I've learned to love everyone so much more, with no expectations, and have found more love from my "real" friends coming back to me. Love is simple, and so often, difficult, yet I know now that the more I love, the more I am loved. What a great lesson, to have so many love you for who you are, simply because you love them that way yourself.

I've learned that humor is a huge part of the journey, and find myself in many "be still my heart" moments when my kids start making fun of and joking about my cancer! Another mission accomplished: I will not allow cancer to rule my life or theirs! And so it hasn't, and we're even closer than ever. The fact that my 12, 16 and 19 year old can laugh about their mom's cancer melts my heart, because I know that they are able to do this because of my attitude, my belief, and my humor, and I'd like to believe, that as a parent, I've helped subside much of their fear of this illness. That's something every parent tries to do, since the day their children are born: kiss away the boo-boo's and take away the fear. I feel so good knowing I've been able to do that for my babies. I know they still have a certain feeling of fear, yet most days, you'd never know!

Lessons…cancer lessons, life lessons, love lessons…all one in the same. You don't need to have cancer to learn more about yourself. You need an open mind, an open heart, and the will to want to change; the want to have a better life, both in your mind, body and soul. I've been learning lessons and changing for years, especially the last several years, so I won't give cancer the entire reason I'm learning and changing now, but I will give the cancer this: you definitely gave me more food for thought, and more reasons I chose to change, but you are NOT the reason I changed. I won't give cancer the power in any way, shape or form, but I will love it while it's here for the experience I'm going through which has allowed me to change, and to change for the better.

Who knew…you CAN change no matter your age! Life is good, my friends, and once again, I begin my day grateful, and tonight I will end my day the very same: grateful!

"It's Like An Arranged Marriage"

September 7, 2013

I don't know if it's the cancer, the chemo, or just me, but I've been full of analogies about my cancer lately. Most of my analogies are humorous and comical, and this latest analogy is no exception.

Having been through two marriages, both ending in divorce, I decided that my breast cancer is somewhat like a bad marriage, except this marriage wasn't by choice…it just happened into my life with no warning, as if it were predetermined to show up when it did.

Here's how I decided to find some humor in my cancer today: My breast cancer is an "arranged marriage" that I had no say in, and no choice to do it. Yet now, I've found my voice and my will and decided that I don't want to be in this bad marriage, so I'm divorcing it. I'll keep this divorce as amicable as I can, and will go through chemo, which is similar to going to a divorce attorney and handling mounds of paperwork, until the six months of chemo are up and the divorce can be finalized early next year. I'm hoping that the cancer doesn't contest this divorce, and that after this six month period, I'll get my final order: cancer free.

So for now, I'm having an "in-house" separation with my breast cancer. We can live together, and can still love one another for now, yet it's not a match made to last a lifetime. Let's get this divorce done "together" for the good of all those involved, and end it on a happy note. The cancer can be gone from my body and I can go on with my own life.

"Behind the Wheel at Wall Stadium!"

September 8, 2013

I spent all four years of high school in the stands of Wall Stadium every Saturday night, hoping to get a free pass into the pits. That never happened. It would be many years later, 2012 to be exact, that I became a journalist for the Wall Revue and was given a weekly "pit pass" to interview the drivers. It was a dream come true! Yet, I always had my own "need for speed" and my own desire to race on that track. That dream came true on August 24th when I received an email the night before from one of the factory stock drivers, asking if I would drive her car in the Powder Puff race the next day. I think I stopped breathing for a brief moment, and immediately emailed her back one word: "Absolutely!"

She and I spoke by phone on Saturday morning, and she said that she and friend, Rob, thought of me while fixing her original car, the Orange Crush. I interviewed Tiffany at the beginning of this season, and as I've told her, she was one of my most impressive interviews. She's a young lady with a heart of gold and extremely talented, spending her days designing websites and her nights working on her car and building her own engines. Throughout the weeks, Tiffany and I became friends.

I got to the track on Saturday about 3pm. Everyone in the pits were so excited knowing I was going to finally fulfill my dream of racing! They asked how I was feeling. My answer was that I was about to throw up and chemo scared me less than driving a race car! They all offered great words of advice and encouragement, yet it was Tiffany and Rob that truly calmed my nerves.

Both Tiffany and Rob got me all suited up, and their main focus was "don't ride the brakes, go for it, and have a good time!" My nervousness increased when they told me there was a slight problem with the Orange Crush and that I'd be driving Tiffany's new car for the season, the 77X!

They got me all strapped into the car for practice, gave me instructions on what to do, and sent me through the pits to hit the track. That first drive down the ramp onto the track was unbelievable, and all I could think of was "here I am, doing something I always wanted to do!" The practice started, and while I was cautious, and probably not driving as fast as most, I had a ball. I pulled back to

WAKING UP

their spot in the pits, hopped out of the car, sat on the window, and never stopped smiling. It was the most amazing feeling I've ever had. How many people fulfill a dream like that?

The night wore on, and I knew the Powder Puff would be around 10pm. I was exhausted, but it was such an exciting night for us all! I ran down into the pits and we had to race, literally, to get me suited up again! Rob hopped in the car with me as I drove to the line-up on the grid, making sure that I was safely strapped in. Tiffany met us there, camera in hand, taking a million pictures. I can't begin to thank the two of them enough for what they did for me. I wondered at times who was more excited, me or them? I knew it had to be me!

The race lasted 15 laps, and was amazing. Now I know how it feels for the drivers I interview to drive down that ramp, wave up to the fans in the stands, and begin driving under the lights. Just to hear your name and car # announced is exciting, and when that green light goes on the dream begins!

I did my best, and even though I didn't win, I won catching a dream! I pulled back into the pits where Tiffany and Rob were waiting for me. I was beyond excited, and they added to that when they told me that they had the video camera on in the car the whole time to tape my race, but didn't want to tell me that in case I got nervous! What more could I ask for?

Racing was great, and hanging out, still in the fire suit with all the other drivers was just as good! It was strange being one of "them" for a brief time, when I'm usually the one interviewing them to find out why they race. Now I know! This experience made me a better writer, a better journalist, and I'm sure my future interviews will have a different style of questions.

What an exciting night, and to be among the "best of the best" of that track will be a memory to last a lifetime for me! Tiffany and Rob are two of the sweetest people I know, and I'm still in awe at what they did for me, and what great care they took of me.

ANNE DENNISH

Sunday morning I woke up to emails from them of all the pictures they took and of my "racing debute video!" Words cannot thank them enough for what they did for me, and for what everyone else in the Wall Stadium Family did.

Dreams come true; you just have to believe, and this Need for Speed girls' dream came true while "Behind the Wheel" at Wall Stadium Speedway.

"Charlotte's Web...Make that Anne's Web!"

September 14, 2013

"Oh what a tangled web we weave, when chemo decides that our hair should leave!" Yup, it's happening, my hair is falling out. I knew the chances were good, but it still was a bit of a shock.

I woke up Wednesday morning, brushed my teeth, and ran my fingers through my hair instead of taking a brush to it. Whoa, there's a bunch of strands through my fingers! Surely this must be a fluke. So, I did it again, and again, and again. No fluke; a fact. I could feel a tingling on my head, and knew right at that moment, it was beginning. Then I realized it was in the sink, on the floor, on my pillow, my keyboard, and on and around anything and anywhere else I was near. Was I ready for this? No, not at all. I sobbed a bit off and on throughout the morning, then took a two-hour nap. When I woke up, I thought that as much as I hated to lose my hair, I hated the mess it was making which I'd have to constantly clean. So, I called my hair salon and made an appointment with my hairdresser, Mark, who's been doing my hair for 20 years. The next day would be the day: another change on the journey.

In the meantime, I knew I had to accept what was happening and find some humor in it. Who knew that humor would be found in my car! I drove my son, Noah, to the track, windows open, chatting away. Suddenly, he started loudly saying "Oh, my God, there's stuff all over me! There must be cob webs in the car!" I looked over at him and at that moment he looked at me and said "Oh my God, Mom, it's your hair!" Ok, who wouldn't laugh? I finally found my humor! It was true.... strands of my hair were flying in the car, sticking to both of us! No, I'm not losing it in clumps, but in strands. Thank God I have thick hair, and lots of it. Well, the two of us started cracking up, and that's when I said, "Well, sweetie, guess it Anne's Web!" Sorry, Charlotte, I'm stealing your line!

The next day my girlfriend and I hit the hairdressers. She took pictures throughout the process, and was crying. I told her to save the tears, because now I had a really short, cute, sexy haircut to hold me for awhile until it all falls out. And I knew if I didn't like the cut, I wouldn't have to worry for long. Truth be told, I love the cut, and I know that when it starts growing back in time, this is the new look I want.

I'm lucky. I've felt really good, have had no nausea, and can do all the things I did before chemo, and I intend to keep it that way even after the next treatment. I'm still being a mom, a smart ass, a writer, a friend, and business woman. Cancer and chemo are not, and will not take that.

So, as I head to Wall Stadium today, I do so with a short, boppy haircut, and a smile stretched across my face. As luck would have it, it's a windy day today, so strands will literally be blowing in the winds of the pits, but the upside it this: I have a Wall Stadium baseball cap that looks really cute with the short hair! All is right with my world today, and in the words of Charlotte, "humble, terrific, radiant!" And yes, I'm humbled by the support of wonderful friends, feeling physically terrific, and looking pretty radiant with my new haircut!

"The Breast Cancer Club"

October 1, 2013

Breast cancer is a club which no one wants to be in or asks to be in. You're placed in it out of nowhere, with no rhyme or reason as to why. I'm one of those girls, yet since I've become a member I have realized that I am in good company with women of strength and courage, of positive energy, of a will that says "I'm gonna kick cancer's ass!"

Breast cancer affects 1 in 8 women, and while I've never considered myself to be "special," well, I guess I am now! I'm the 1 out of the 8 to have breast cancer, and the other 7 are missing out on all the fun of having it! (And yes, I say that sarcastically!"

Life get's very busy for all of us, between home, family, work, and life in general, that we tend to forget about taking care of ourselves. I was one of those people, and didn't have a mammogram over five years. Part of the reason I'm passionate about being so open with my breast cancer is because "I don't want my journey to become someone else's journey." Early detection is so important, and I hope that through my writing, my voice, my willingness to share my story with others, that I can make a difference in even just one woman's life. In the words of John Lennon: "life is what happens when we're busy making other plans."

I was diagnosed in July, and have already undergone two chemo treatments. I'm lucky not to have nausea, thanks to some amazing drugs I take to prevent it. I thought that I'd be sick all the time, yet I haven't. I still cook, clean, do laundry and cart the kids around, still write my column and hang at the track, still function as if I don't have cancer. Life seems just like it was, but there's that "elephant" in the room, which for me is that port on my chest and the wig on my dresser that reminds me every day that I do have breast cancer.

I'm handling my cancer with a sense of humor, grace, dignity, and a positive attitude! I've always considered myself a strong woman, yet now, my strength amazes even me. I may have a moment here and there when I just want to cry and say "no more, I've had enough, I want to be normal;" yet for right now, this is my normal. This is my life.

I don't look at cancer as being something terrible that happened to me. I won't lie, I would not have chosen to have it, but since I do, I want to make a difference with it. I want to support, enlighten, and encourage other women going through this. I don't want my cancer to be in vain, and I'm a big believer that everything happens for a reason. My cancer is no exception. Since being diagnosed, I have met some amazing people, had some unexpected opportunities fall into my life, and have been able to see people for their true colors. Most of the people in my life shine like a rainbow, and I've made so many new friends and found my greatest support in places I would have never imagined.

My choice is this: that for anything good or bad that happens in my life, I will see the good in it and try to do something good with it. I'm blessed to be a writer, and it's time I used my writing as my voice for breast cancer.

I'm not a pro at cancer, as unfortunately so many women are, yet these are the women teaching me, and guiding me throughout this journey. I want to be just like them; they are in inspiration. I want to do something positive for myself, for my children, for all the other women fighting the battle, for the women who won, and in memory of the women who lost.

Cancer changes your perspective on life, all for the good. It's filled with many challenges, yet it's filled with many lessons. I embrace every challenge, and am grateful for every lesson I've learned so far. Take care of yourselves, be smart, and please, for all of us who are fighting this disease, who have survived it, and who have lost the fight: "don't let our journey become yours."

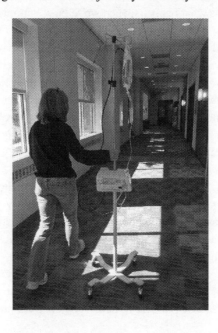

"Breast Cancer... The Time Warp"

October 13, 2013

Breast cancer is a glitch in time, a bump in the road of your life. My hope is that when my chemo is done, and whatever surgery is necessary, it will simply become a "time warp" in my life. A moment when we can all say "I am a survivor" and the time we spent fighting cancer will be just a "time warp."

When I was first diagnosed in July, all I could think about was what a disruption to my life this would be, of all the time I would lose to treat this cancer and become a survivor. Yet strangely, I don't see it that way anymore. True, it is a bit of a disruption, but I will not let it stop my life. It may change my life for a brief time, but it will not stop it! So, repeat after me: CANCER WILL NOT STOP MY LIFE, IT WILL JUST CHANGE IT FOR AWHILE!

I don't kid myself into thinking that my lifestyle hasn't changed a bit, but then again, change can be a good thing. Cancer, for most of us will change our appearance, and again, this is only for a brief period of time. For me, my first thought was that I'd be going through this for at least a year or two, but in the grand scheme of life, that's not such a long time. It's a time to change and a time to learn. Life with or without cancer is always changing, and I for one embrace all changes in my life, good or bad, because I've learned through experience that even through the bad times, more good experiences with so much more happiness and joy came into my life.

I've decided to take this "time warp" and make the most of it. It's time to find a new "me" in how I look; a look I feel confident, beautiful, and yes, even "sexy" with! Cancer can't rob you of feeling good about yourself; only you can allow it to do that. Why not decide, at this moment, on this day, to continue to fight the cancer, but to fight for yourself as a woman more! "Attitude is everything," and that's not just for "fighting the disease" anymore. Attitude is about how we feel about ourselves, both inside and out, and if we can find our comfort zone of being a woman, fighting the cancer becomes so much easier to do. Feel sexy, feel beautiful, feel bad-ass...feel whatever makes you feel good. Re-invent the body you have while fighting cancer, into the woman who fights it with grace, dignity, beauty, and even a new sense of style!

Today I decided to be that woman I was before cancer. I went shopping at my favorite lingerie store and bought my favorite perfume, a few "girlie" things," then on to buy my sexy smelling bath wash. I finished up with a trip to the store for some new clothes. Three small things that reminded me of what it feels like to feel like a woman! Take that, cancer!

Keep kickin' cancers' ass, and while you're at it, feel free to do it with a sexy looking outfit and some spiked heels! You'll feel better, and soon enough, when you have become a survivor, you won't have to "jump to the left" anymore: you can take that time warp and "step to the right...right into being a survivor!"

"Home is Where..."

October 25, 2013

Home is where my children are, where I can sit outside and look up at a star filled sky or bask in the sunlight, where I can sit on my laptop and find my creativity. Home is where my heart is, and that "home" isn't always a specific place.

My home can be dining out in a restaurant with my friends, or having coffee on the boardwalk thinking about my life, or "my home" can be found deep in my thoughts about those I love, those I think about, and those I miss. I love "my home" because it's where I find my peace, where I can close my eyes and let my thoughts turn into memories of wonderful moments that are simply memories now.

Home is my comfort zone, and I can find it anywhere, anytime, if I only think about it and open my heart to all that is, all that it was, and all that is to be. Home is my strength when I'm feeling weak, my happiness when I'm feeling sad, my place to go when loneliness shakes me to my toes and I need to remember the times I wasn't lonely…the times I wasn't alone. Home is where I go to remember when life was easier, simpler, and the place I go to look forward to where life is going to take me.

My home is the sounds of my children telling me their dreams, of the laughter of those I love, of the stories that strangers share with me. Home is a place that no one can take away from me; that no one can creep into and upset. "My home" is my guarded, sacred space; a place where only I can be. It is a place without fear, without heartache, without worry. It is a place filled with love.

Some may think my home is a dream world, a "place" I make up in my mind. Perhaps to some it is, maybe even to myself at times. Yet "my home" is where I think, where I wander in my thoughts, where I "see" all that I want in my life and release it to the Heavens to be certain it comes to fruition. It's the place where every wonderful, loving, fun memory I have is safely guarded and well protected from harm's way.

Home is where my heart is and my heart is everywhere. You'll find it in my children, my friends, my family and in my writing. "Home" is everything that I am, everything that I was, and everything that I want to become.

"My home is my heart."

"If These Wigs Could Talk"

November 1, 2013

It's a funny feeling to getting used to wearing a wig, yet it's also my saving grace. While some women are comfortable in being bald, I'm not. Well, to be fair, the only time my wig is off is when I'm home, and even then, I have a baseball hat on. I'm thankful every day for this sexy little hair that a wonderful, sweet wigmaker suggested for me. It's a style I love, and may just keep when my hair does grow back in.

As I'm writing this, I'm thinking of all the people I see at chemo wearing their wigs. I'm wondering if their wig prevented them from life or enhanced their life? I know for me, I've talked to some and heard what they've to say. I thought it would make a great story one day about what these wigs would have say "if they could talk!"

People on the outside don't always understand, yet while going through the daily task of wearing a wig, these people would be amazed at what these wigs would say.

So, with that I write a few funny things that some of the other cancer patients and I shared about our funny stories.

If my wig could talk, it would say:

- That I went on the best cruise with my family, and my wig had a ball!

- That I made mad, passionate love last night and my wig stayed on!

- My girlfriend and I went out dancing, and no matter how much we danced, that wig stayed on! It bopped all over, but never left my head!

- My wig loves driving in a convertible!

- My wig went to my horseback riding lesson!

- That I went to work every day, and no one knew it was a wig!

- More people ask me now where I get my hair done than when I had hair!

- I drove on a motorcycle!

- I fell in love.

- I played Frisbee with my kids.

- **"My wig would say that I was there to get you through a rough time, to make you feel pretty, and to make you realize that you can be or do anything you want with me on your head."**

Final note: I love my wig!

"The Surgery"

February 25, 2014

My surgery was just a few days ago, on February 21st to be exact, and what a day it was. I thank God for my cousin, who took me to have it done. She came over before 5am, with a tray of lasagna for when I got home. We hopped into the car and took the 45 minute drive to the hospital. We got there and so began the preparation for surgery.

It's funny, my tumor had shrunk completely, yet the tissue around where it had been needed to be removed, along with the tissue on the upper part of my breast where some calcifications had been. The surgeon was hoping to remove no more than 3 lymph nodes. Needless to say, I was thankful for this second opinion I opted for, because while the first doctor wanted to do a double mastectomy, I found myself on surgery day only having a lumpectomy.

I won't go in to all the details of the surgery preparations because, quite frankly, they weren't fun. After an hour of a mammogram which tried to insert two long wires into my clips and a shot in my breast for which I could not be numbed, well, you can see why I'd rather not write about it. Trust me, the memory of that day will never leave me…not ever. It was a day that made me realize just how strong such a feminine body of a woman can be. We can endure pain which is indescribable and still come out okay.

It was time to hop into my bed and wait for the surgeon to come in and autograph the breast that needed the surgery. As I lay there waiting, I began thinking about every little thing that had happened to me throughout this journey since it began, and what it all meant today. Two people who were friends walked out on me the day of the surgery; they never looked back and neither did I. The true colors of friends and family had shown through, and although it was hurtful to me, I was okay with it all.

So, after one more quick run to the bathroom, I wheeled my IV stand back down to my bed, dancing the entire way down the hallway. This was the end, at least most of it, and I couldn't wait.

The surgeon came in, signed my breast, and as I was wheeled down to the operating room, I looked up at him and said: "If I give you a few names, can you cut them out of me along with that breast tissue?" He laughed, I was serious. So, as I entered the room and the medication began kicking in, I silently cut them out in my mind.

I woke up in recovery with a blue, floral and ruffled compression band, which looked like a 1970's tube top. How could you not laugh? The surgeon came, told me it went extremely well, and that he only had to remove two lymph nodes. A sigh relief was an understatement.

We drove home and my cousin dropped me off, making sure I got in alright. My mom had cleaned for me all day, and my three boys were the only ones home when I got there. Aside from the delicious and much needed dinner my cousin had made, the only other thing I came home to was a beautiful vase of flowers… which I had ordered the day before for myself. I knew I wanted fresh flowers when I came home, and I knew there would be no one to send them to me, so I ordered them myself. I told the girls at the florist to sign the card for me, and be sure they were at my house before I got home.

Surgery day went well, and there was nothing better than coming home to my kids, a tray of lasagna, and MY flowers. Now, let's wait for the results of the surgery…

"53 and Cancer-Free!"

March 15, 2014

I've been too busy to write, and quite frankly, most of this chapter is ending just as planned. The surgery was a great success; "it went better than most of this nature," my surgeon told me. What a great day that was. So, I decided that the day of my surgery, February 21st, would be my anniversary date.

It's my birthday today, and three of my girlfriends and I are going out to celebrate at my favorite restaurant. We've decided to call this birthday "53 and Cancer-Free!"

Life is good today, and I am forever grateful that the surgery went so well. I still have to have a treatment of Herceptin every 3 weeks until this November, and some radiation in a few weeks, but hey, I can live with that…and I am!

Onward to my night tonight!

"Last Day of Radiation"

May 15, 2014

I decided to do a three week clinical trial of radiation, so for those three weeks, I took that 45 minute drive each way to have it done. I was terrified of the whole idea of radiation, yet I knew it was one of the final pieces. I made it fun while I was there, joking with the nurses, helping them pick out bathing suits for the upcoming summer season at the shore. It was a bit sad to say good-bye on that last day, but I had them all sign my journal, just as I had had every other nurse sign throughout every procedure, every treatment.

I remember my radiologist asking me on the first day of radiation, what I thought of it…he wanted to know if it was as bad as I thought it would be. I thought for a second and answered him with: "No, it reminded me of the first time you have sex. It's quick, not that big of a deal, and not anything like what you had expected." He laughed and said he'd be using that line on his future patients!

The last day was on May 5th, that time of year when all the towns begin "Paint the Town Pink." I swore I'd never be a "pink" girl, yet as I drove through the towns decorated to the hills with ribbons and everything pink you could imagine, I couldn't help but feel like they did it just for me. I know they didn't, but I finally realized why it's so important to some. To me, it was the perfect day to celebrate the end radiation, and begin to move on in life.

As I write this, I will say that I have said "good bye" to my wig. My hair is now a length I could get colored and live with, so it was out with that style, and now in with a very, short look. It's the new me, and I like her. She seems smarter and stronger for all she had just gone through…and that is "me."

ANNE DENNISH

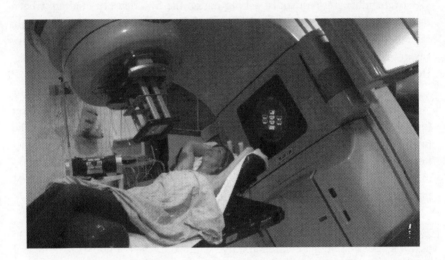

"Last Treatment"

November 17th, 2014

I just had my last Herceptin treatment a few hours ago. I drove myself up there and spent the last hours with my amazing chemo nurses. They were the best in the world, and taught me more about this journey than any doctor could have. They were the ones' that told me early on that the women who have the best chance of survival are the ones' that know their body and do what's best for it. And I was one of them.

So, as the nurses trekked in throughout the last round of herceptin, they signed my journal and gave me lots of hugs. I took pictures of everything, and when the buzzer on the IV went off that it was finished, the curtain blew open with a rush of confetti and all those crazy nurses I had learned to love as family! They were laughing and crying, as was I, and gave me a sign to hold up for a picture… "hip hip hooray, treatment ends today!" I'll always love them for that.

I'm home now, celebrating this day with my children. Like they told me: "we knew you'd be fine, Mom." Then off they went! I'm glad it's over, and I'm glad I'm a survivor. One more piece…port removal!

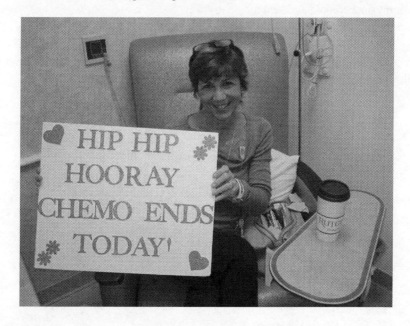

"My Port-O-Call Girl"

November 20, 2014

It's done…she's gone. I so lovingly nicknamed my port "my port-o-call girl!" As much as I didn't like that thing in my chest, she made my life throughout this journey extremely easy, and for that I will be forever grateful.

I was at the hospital this morning with my dad, and while getting prepped to go in I asked my nurse this question: "How do most people feel about getting their ort out?" She stood there looking at me, and told me no one ever asked her that. I told her it was bittersweet for me, after all, this thing had been in my body for over a year and a half, and while I'm glad it's to get it out, it's going to feel weird not having that bump there. She understood, and thought that she would start asking patients that.

I was wheeled in, and only given a local around the area! I was so hoping for at least a twilight sleep, but no, just a local. I chatted with the doctor while she split me open and took it out. I told her to clean it up because I wanted to take it home. She told me they don't usually do that, and I told her that they do today! So, as she and the tech laughed at me, they cleaned up my port, closed me up, hid it in my pocketbook, and sent me on my way.

It's all done. The journey is over. I'm sitting home now in awe of this ending, in complete gratitude to God and my Angels that I made it through, and that it's all over. The cancer is gone and all the treatments down. Now what?

"Now What?"

December 1, 2014

You go through almost two years of treatment, then it's all gone and over with. What do you do now?

I feel like I'm breathing normally again, yet since having had cancer, there's always that slight worry in the back of my mind that it may come back. There's always that reminder when I see my three scars. Yet, I know what happens next is all up to me.

It's time to move forward, remembering all that I learned. It's time to write another book. It's time help someone else get through this. It's time for everything and anything!

Nothing will stop me or slow me down. Life is too short to waste any time. Forget drama and stress; it's no longer welcome in my world. I learned to love and care for myself, and I know that will spill onto those around me.

I know where my life with cancer took me; I'm excited to see where life without it will take me now!

"Gratitude with Attitude!

"And in the end, the love you take is equal to the love you make..."

~The Beatles~

"Fits Like a Glove"

For the first time in more years than I can count, I'm in a life that fits like a glove; a life that took me by surprise and allowed me to be exactly who I am. It's funny how up until now I thought I was being "myself," yet in the last several months my life changed in more ways than I could imagine, and along with my life, my whole self seemed to change right along with it.

There was no defining moment, no fanfare, no particular moment of the change, just a morning of sitting outside alone with the sunrise that I sat and let my mind be still. It was then that all the blessings in my life came to light, and as I started counting them I realized that this new happiness and peace came from many changes, some good, some not so good, but changes that brought me to exactly where I am now: happy, content, and in love.

Life has a way of happening when we least expect it. People come and go, finances change, our children grow up and move out, yet in the midst of all these changes, "life" found me. I sat and thought about how things had changed, but my thoughts kept coming back to where I am now. I guess that in the end it doesn't always matter how we got here, it's a blessing that we did. Sometimes when we're not looking for something we want, it finds us all on its' own. It's that "waking up" moment of taking stock of your life and realizing that you are exactly where you should be, and where you always wanted to be; that moment that you sit and think about everything and are suddenly overwhelmed with emotion because you realize "wow, this life I'm in fits me like a glove!" And for me, that's a foreign concept.

I've spent many years of this life enduring the good and the bad, each chapter of my life different from the one before, and thinking that each new one was the life I was supposed to be in. Yet today, I know that life right at this moment is much different than the other chapters in my book of life. This chapter isn't the last one, but the first one of a new section of my book. This chapter is filled with the knowledge of all the lessons in which I've learned so much about myself, and how a life that I've always wanted found me. It found me in the middle of a snowy winter at the shore, and it finds me now in the heat of the summer. It finds me every morning, and sleeps alongside of me at night. It fills my daydreams and dances through my night dreams. It touches my heart and soul in places I never knew existed. It fills me with laughter and holds me tight with love.

ANNE DENNISH

This life was meant for me, and I've never witnessed something so extraordinary as my life today. It's as if God and the Universe got together and lined things up to as near perfection as possible. Every experience and person that have come into this new life were lined up like a row of dominoes, yet as each domino falls, it's not with malice or contempt, it's with love and hope. I trust each fall of every one, because I know with all that I am that this is how it's supposed to be. The trials and tribulations I've endured throughout my life have brought a bounty of blessings into my life, and to the lives of those around me. For the first time I'm truly able to see how everything that has happened and that every person that entered my world did so for a reason and a purpose. There are no accidents, and there are none in my world now.

Some days I sit in sheer amazement at how perfectly everything is happening and how quickly things are moving. Life seems to move too slowly at times, yet at this time in my life things are moving at a pace so quickly at times that I believe life is in a hurry to get me to where it wants me to be. There are moments during a mundane day of housework and bills that I think to myself "what a great little life I'm in!" It's as near perfection as I could want or have ever hoped for.

These changes are not anything I would have thought were to happen in my life. I find myself in situations that I never would have thought possible and loving people that I thought would be an impossible task to do. Friendships have sparked out of the blue, and while they may have seemed as though a loyalty between the two wouldn't exist, it does. It can be overwhelming at times, a moment filled with the emotions of love and peace, but I'll gratefully accept it. It seems I've been searching and waiting for this all along, and throughout all these years, I began to believe that where I am now only existed in books and fairy tales. I began to accept that this "fit like a glove" feeling in my life wasn't really true; it was simply a fantasy to me that I wrote about. I used to believe that if I couldn't "live" it, I could certainly "write" it.

Yet here I find myself writing about my fairy tale that has become my reality. Dreams do come true, and my best advice is that when you can love yourself unconditionally, respect yourself for all that you are, and place a value on yourself deserving of all good things, then others will, too. Once you accept all "that is," all that "will be" suddenly finds its' way to your door.

"Never say never," because what you believe to be true today can suddenly change tomorrow. What you thought would never happen, may happen next week, and just when you thought life would "never fit like a glove," the Universe hands you a pair more comfortable than any other you've ever worn.

Don't be afraid of life changing, because sometimes what we know to be true turns out to have not been true at all. Take a leap of faith in yourself and in your Higher Power, because in the end it's not always "us" that finds the life we want; it's "life" that brings us the life we so deserve.

"The Lessons of the Adventures"

"If you can't be in a good relationship with yourself first, you'll never be in a good one with anyone else."

"If you have to tell someone how to love you, you might as well tell them how to leave you."

"Smile through it, laugh at it, then dance around it."

"Home is everything that I am, everything that I was, and everything that I hope to become."

"Never let something get the best of you; go get the best of something."

"Every new day brings the chance to do it better than the day before."

"If you're going to love someone, be sure you can tell them why."

"The best relationships to be in are the ones that bring out the best in you."

"The only way to open the door to your future is to close the doors to your past."

"While the words are good to hear, it's the actions that make them truth."

"Trials, tribulations and blessings are one in the same. You can't have one without the other."

"Failure is staying within your comfort zone; success is stepping out of it."

"A dreamer is a realist with faith."

"Forget who you were; decide who you are."

"There are always differences between people; embrace them or replace them."

"Life is too short and unpredictable to be anything less than happy."

"While you're busy feeding someone's ego, they're busy starving your self-esteem."

"Sometimes we have to do something uncomfortable to become comfortable."

"At one time or another we have to revisit our past, if only to remind us why we left it there to begin with."

"Sometimes what we think is ending never really had a beginning at all."

"A broken heart is proof that is still works."

"The truth is free; lies will cost you a price."

"If you're not willing to love yourself unconditionally, why would you expect anyone else to do it for you?"

"It takes but one moment of ignorance to cost you a lifetime of bliss."

"Everything can be forgiven, yet not everything can be repaired."

"Letting go is the only way of moving forward."

"You can't move forward if you're standing still."

"With faith there is hope; with fear there is nothing."

"When you can't find the strength, let the strength find you."

"Going through tough times doesn't make you stronger; it makes you realize just how strong you were all along."

"The ultimate test of trust is love."

"There is no dancing in the dark, only in the light."

"Fear prevents you from moving forward; intuition let's you know it's safe."

"When you can't get over something, go around it!"

ANNE DENNISH

"There are times I like not knowing where I'm going; it makes it so much more exciting when I get there."

"It's funny that the moment you stop looking for something is the very moment you find it."

"When one door closes, let the French doors open"

"True happiness comes from within, not from without."

"The wrong person wants something FROM you; the right person wants everything FOR you!"

"The heart see's the truth of what the eyes cannot."

"The greatest lesson of being with the WRONG person is that we learn how to see what the RIGHT person looks like."

"It isn't worth your time if it doesn't make you shine."

"Every girl needs a best girlfriend who can make her laugh so hard that she wants to pee her pants!"

"If you should find yourself getting hit hard with the truth, at least let it knock some sense into you."

"Look inward instead of outward; look up instead of down; and look forward instead of backwards."

"In order to know the truth, you must go to the source."

"Sometimes the smartest thing to do is the hardest thing to do."

"We don't become who we are by chance; we become who we are by choice."

"If you want to go through life with just a carry-on, then you must first be willing to throw away your baggage."

"I used to believe that you should trust everyone until they give you a reason not to; I've since learned that you should trust people when they earn it."

"When you've finally had enough of something and have hit your wall, it's time to start looking for the door."

"The best smile to see on someone's face is born from the smile in their heart."

"Sometimes life takes an unexpected turn, sending us on the journey of a lifetime. We may not end up where we dreamed, but we will always end of where we belong."

"And I am finally where I belong..."

~Anne Dennish~

"Before I say good-bye..."

Thank you for taking the time to read "Waking Up." It was a book born from deep within my heart, and while my life is far from perfect, I wanted to share all that I've learned with you. I'm hoping that it made you smile, touched your heart, and made you feel good about yourself.

Life is meant to be lived to the fullest each and every day, and my wish for you is that no matter what type of day you're having, you'll find a glimmer of hope, a reason to smile, and something to laugh at.

I wish you love and light, joy and happiness; today and always!

WAKING UP

Thank you with all my heart,

~Anne Dennish~

For more information you may visit: www.annedennish.com

Printed in the United States
By Bookmasters